Coping with Mandates

MICHAEL FIX
DAPHNE KENYON
Editors

Ann Calvaresi Barr
David R. Beam
James L. Blum
Anthony V. D'Aiello
Theresa A. Gullo
Richard H. Horte
Janet M. Kelly
Arnold M. Kuzmack
Emily D. Lunceford
Geary Maher

Coping with Mandates

What Are the Alternatives?

ATLANTIC COMM. COLLEGE

THE URBAN INSTITUTE PRESS
Washington, D.C.

THE URBAN INSTITUTE PRESS
2100 M Street, N.W.
Washington, D.C. 20037

Library of Congress Cataloging in Publication Data
    Coping with Mandates: What Are the Alternatives?
1. Intergovernmental fiscal relations—United States.   2. Federal government—
United States.   3. Local finances—law and legislation.   I. Fix, Michael.
II. Kenyon, Daphne A.
KF6720.C66   1989   343.73'034—dc20   89-28319
                                                                                                                            CIP

ISBN 0-87766-435-8 (alk. paper)
ISBN 0-87766-434-X (alk. paper; casebound)

Urban Institute books are printed on acid-free paper whenever possible.

Printed in the United States of America.

9   8   7   6   5   4   3   2   1

Distributed by
            University Press of America
4720 Boston Way   3 Henrietta Street
Lanham, MD 20706   London WC2E 8LU ENGLAND

THE URBAN INSTITUTE is a nonprofit policy research and educational organization established in Washington, D.C., in 1968. Its staff investigates the social and economic problems confronting the nation and government policies and programs designed to alleviate such problems. The Institute disseminates significant findings of its research through the publications program of its Press. The Institute has two goals for work in each of its research areas: to help shape thinking about societal problems and efforts to solve them, and to improve government decisions and performance by providing better information and analytic tools.

Through work that ranges from broad conceptual studies to administrative and technical assistance, Institute researchers contribute to the stock of knowledge available to public officials and private individuals and groups concerned with formulating and implementing more efficient and effective government policy.

Conclusions or opinions expressed in Institute publications are those of the authors and do not necessarily reflect the views of other staff members, officers or trustees of the Institute, advisory groups, or any organizations that provide financial support to the Institute.

ACKNOWLEDGMENTS

The papers on which this volume is based were presented at a conference entitled "Coping with Mandates: What are the Alternatives?" held at The Urban Institute on May 20, 1988. Blaine Liner, the director of The Urban Institute's State Policy Center, initiated the idea of a conference and a published volume of papers. The mandates topic was chosen because the issue was identified as one of the most important current state and local policy issues by the governors making up the Advisory Panel of The Urban Institute's State Policy Center. The J. Howard Pew Freedom Trust provided funding.

Many people deserve thanks for making the conference a success and for realizing the potential of this volume of papers. The conference was put together by Daphne A. Kenyon of The Urban Institute, Ann Calvaresi Barr and Richard Horte of the U.S. General Accounting Office, and Jane Roberts of the Advisory Commission on Intergovernmental Relations. Certain speakers who either did not present papers, or whose remarks could not be included in this volume made important contributions to the conference discussion: Robert Ebel of the Advisory Commission on Intergovernmental Relations, Andrew Card, Jr., of the White House Office of Intergovernmental Affairs, Beverly Bell of Congressman Doug Barnard's Office, and William Gadsby of the U.S. General Accounting Office. Mary Mingo and Martha Nicholson ably managed the conference logistics.

Susan Braman's help was invaluable in putting together the first draft of this volume. Helpful comments on the draft were made by George Peterson, John Shannon, and David Walker.

CONTENTS

Tables

FOREWORD

Federal aid to state and local governments has been shrinking steadily during the 1980s, and many responsibilities that used to be federal ones have reverted back to the states. Some regulatory requirements have also been lifted but many remain. In this era of fiscal stringency, states look back longingly to what they perceive as a time of federal funding with few constraints. Further, they are expressing concern that the federal government is relying increasingly on regulatory powers to impose its priorities on programs that receive no federal funding. This nostalgia and this fear of being shackled by unfunded mandates are the main features of the current public debate on mandates.

The issue is, however, a complex one. First, mandates, by which the authors mean regulations that one level of government imposes on another, are not just a federal–state issue; they also affect state–local relations. Indeed, many of the new approaches to mandating during the 1980s have involved state regulation of local activities. Second, even at the federal level, mandating of some type is not unprecedented. But the vast majority of federal relations governing state actions are not unfunded mandates, but conditions of financial assistance. These vary widely in how constraining they are to state action and how large the program funds are that they supply. Even in the 1960s and 1970s, however, when federal grants-in-aid were rapidly increasing, unrestricted aid never amounted to more than a small fraction of total federal aid to states and localities.

Nonetheless, mandating became a far more pressing concern to state–local and federal policymakers in the past ten years than in prior decades. In this volume Michael Fix, Daphne Kenyon, and their contributing authors examine the mandates issue in light of both the history of mandates and the recent experience of federal and state governments in responding to complaints from lower jursidictions about mandates. One of the achievements of the book is to place the mandating issue within three larger contexts: the policy goals that intergovernmental regulations are intended to achieve (e.g., a cleaner environment or safer communities), the inevitable tensions among the three planes of government in the American federal system, and the evolving assessment of regulation as a tool of government policy. Another is to describe and assess the effectiveness of cost estimation and mandate reimbursement as means to cope with mandates. Case studies from the state level (Connecticut, Massachusetts, and South Carolina) and the federal level (Office of Drinking Water, Environmental Protection Agency) provide valuable examples of mandates and the difficulties mandates present.

Studying the interaction among different levels of government, and laws and practices that contribute to the greater good of the nation and its citizens, is an important part of the Institute's work. We hope that the discussion in these pages will help diffuse some of the heat that now surrounds the issue, and that a more informed debate will, in turn, lead to more responsive government at all levels.

William Gorham
President

INTRODUCTION

Michael Fix and Daphne A. Kenyon

In popular usage, a mandate is an order or command. Within the world of intergovernmental relations, it has come to stand for a set of regulations that one level of government imposes on another—regulations that have generated a host of political complaints about their costs and intrusiveness. Intergovernmental mandates include three basic regulatory tools: unfunded mandates, or regulations for which no direct aid is provided; conditions attached to the receipt of intergovernmental aid; and the conscription of states into administering national regulatory programs.

At the heart of the mandating issue is an old set of federalism questions: where in the intergovernmental system should policy be made, who should be charged with its implementation, and who should pay the costs of compliance? The issue is not just an artifact of federal–state relations; it reflects tensions in the relationship of states to their own political subdivisions. After all, it is at the state level where some of the most innovative approaches to the mandates issue are being developed.

The purpose of this volume—which brings together papers presented at a conference held at The Urban Institute in May 1988—is to explore the emergence and early history of the mandating issue, to examine the state and federal policy responses to the complaints about mandating, and to identify the lessons of those policy experiments.

EMERGENCE OF THE MANDATING ISSUE

From the Korean War until the late 1970s, federal grants-in-aid to state and local governments grew steadily as a percentage of the federal budget, as a proportion of state and local budgets, and in relation to the GNP. At its peak, there were more than 500 federal aid programs. Most of them provided categorical assistance and were accompanied by a multiplicity of programmatic and administrative requirements. Despite the consensus among state and local policy-makers and academics in favor of block grants or general revenue-sharing funding as opposed to categorical grants-in-aid, such unrestricted aid never amounted to a large fraction of total federal aid to states and localities.

About 1978, a new era in federal–state–local relations began. Federal grants-in-aid, which had grown steadily over the past 20 years, began to shrink. State and local governments accustomed to lobbying Congress for additional assistance were introduced to "Fend-for-Yourself-Federalism." Not only did direct federal aid to state and local governments decline as a proportion of the federal budget, but the Tax Reform Act of 1986 and other federal tax acts reduced indirect aid to state and local governments provided through the federal tax code.

Although federal aid to state and local governments was shrinking significantly, federal regulatory requirements were not being reduced commensurately. Strings remained attached to federal aid. Newer, more coercive forms of intergovernmental regulation were being imposed, and the federal government was still selectively overriding state priorities. New York City Mayor Edward I. Koch, along with other state and local officials, responded by protesting the "mandate millstone." Academics and policy analysts began to examine the issue, and the Advisory Commission on Intergovernmental Relations's study of federal mandates was disseminated in one of its most influential publications, *Regulatory Federalism: Policy, Process, Impact and Reform*.[1]

Today, after a decade of federal retrenchment and selective regulatory relief and with the prospect of unending federal deficits, it is the spectre of unfunded mandates that most concerns state and local officials. They worry that in an era when programmatic change through spending has been ruled out, policymakers will rely increasingly on their regulatory powers to respond to crises and powerful interest groups. And they worry that their governments will either end up being directly regulated or responsible for the costly implementation of another government's regulatory priorities.[2]

As indicated above, mandates are not just a federal–state issue; they also color state–local relations. The emergence of the mandating issue at this state–local level is due to two developments. One was the taxpayers' revolt, which placed revenue restrictions on local governments and made compliance with state-mandated service requirements fiscally painful. The other was the growing prominence of state as opposed to federal policies in a time of federal retrenchment.

DEFINING MANDATES

It is said that providing a proper definition of a problem goes at least half way toward finding a solution. This maxim appears to be more than usually apt in the case of mandates. Three broad types of mandates are identified here: unfunded mandates, conditions of assistance, and the cooperative federal–state regulatory programs referred to as partial preemptions.[3]

Unfunded mandates take three principal forms. The first is *direct orders*. They impose civil or criminal sanctions and do not make compliance contingent on the receipt of federal funds. One example is wastewater treatment standards promulgated under the Clean Water Act.

Another type of intergovernmental regulation that could be considered an unfunded mandate is *crosscutting requirements*. These rules are routinely attached not to one but to all relevant federally funded programs. They typically regulate such areas as financial accounting practices, antidiscrimination, and minimum wage levels. Examples include Title VI of the Civil Rights Act of 1964, which bars discrimination in federally assisted programs, and the Davis–Bacon Act, which sets minimum wage levels on federally assisted construction projects.

A third, comparatively rare, form of unfunded mandate is *crossover sanctions*, which impose penalties in one program area to force compliance in another. A frequently cited example is the Highway Beautification Act of 1965, which threatened to withhold highway construction funds if states did not comply with billboard control standards.

With unfunded mandates, the relationship between federal and state governments is virtually all stick and no carrot. However, a closer examination of intergovernmental regulations reveals the great majority to be *conditions of assistance* and not unfunded mandates. Unlike crosscutting regulations or crossover sanctions, conditions of assistance are directly related to implementing the legislative goals of the program to which they have been attached (e.g., the share of a municipality's bus fleet that must be accessible to the disabled to comply with federal law). These conditions of aid vary widely in the regulatory burdens they impose and the offsetting levels of program support that are provided. Assessing the burden they impose requires taking into account such factors as the share of compliance costs paid by the federal government, the prescriptiveness of the attached conditions, the degree to which those conditions depart from local preferences, and the size, demography, and financial strength of the jurisdiction.

A third, distinct, type of intergovernmental regulatory tool that can be considered a mandate is *partial preemption programs*. Under these schemes, the federal government sets basic standards and can designate specific methods for their attainment. States that agree to meet minimum federal standards and demonstrate the capacity to do so are then delegated authority to take over the programs' day-to-day administration. Although state standards cannot fall below federal standards, the states generally remain free to exceed them; hence, state prerogatives are only *partially preempted* by federal law. If the state chooses to defer to the federal government or if it proves utterly unable to administer a program that conforms to minimum requirements, the federal government assumes responsibility for implementation.

Why should such programs be considered mandates? In the words of one former Environmental Protection Agency official, William Pedersen:

The opportunity to operate some of these [partial preemption] programs is more of an effort to conscript the states into federal service than it is an acknowledgment of their autonomy.[4]

Pedersen goes on to point out that such programs "move more on the level of administrative convenience than on any philosophical level of allocating responsibilities between state and federal governments," and they "effectively turn the states into regional offices of the federal government."[5]

MANDATING: UNDERLYING CONCERNS

At its core, the complex issue of mandating, with the powerful conflicts of interests and values that underlie it, reflects concern over: (1) the distribution of intergovernmental resources, (2) the distribution of intergovernmental responsibilities, (3) the limits of regulation, and (4) goals of the activist social legislation of the 1960s and 1970s that are frequently implemented by mandates.

The Distribution of Resources

The extent to which mandating is a resource issue has already been highlighted. State and local officials feel that, with declining federal aid but growing federal regulation, the federal government is requiring states and localities to do more with less. Furthermore, in the face of continued huge federal deficits, states and localities are concerned that new federal policies may be implemented increasingly through regulation rather than federal spending, leaving the credit for new programs in Washington but shifting the costs to state and local governments.

Fiscal issues also underlie local government concern with state mandating. In this era of budget stringency following widespread taxpayer revolts, the conjunction of mandated service requirements and restrictions on revenue-raising powers makes local government finance more difficult. Not surprisingly, mandate reimbursement laws have been enacted in those same states (e.g., California and Massachusetts) in which the tax revolt has imposed the most severe constraint on local revenue-raising powers.

The Distribution of Responsibilities

Mandating is also an *authority* issue. At one level, we need to ask: who has the legal right to make decisions that bind lower levels of government? It is clear that the states have been big losers in this area as their constitutionally defined zones of autonomy—those areas in which state authority overrides federal authority—have been significantly circumscribed by the Supreme Court.[6]

Beyond the question of right is the political and administrative question of *competence:* who is the most qualified to set policy in a specific policy area? It is ironic that the judicial demise of state sovereignty comes at a time when state budgets and program sophistication are on the rise. These trends also coincide with increased skepticism over the capacity of the federal government to manage complex programs and regulatory regimes. The difficulty of reconciling the states' new capabilities and the federal government's changing role has led to intergovernmental tension—tension reflected in the states' restiveness over continuing to serve as the field hands of federalism.

Equity is another issue. Mandates permit higher levels of government to take credit for distributing benefits through the society while
they often leave the costs of paying for those benefits to lower levels
of government. At the same time, the advocates of new mandates
can take political credit for aiding interest groups while they retain
the authority to intervene in program operations and shift the blame
for program failure to lower levels of government.[7]

The Effectiveness of Regulation

The mandating issue must also be seen in the context of the ongoing
debate over deregulation. After all, it is in this light that the mandates
issue was cast politically during the Reagan administration. Intergovernmental regulations were some of the most visible and vaunted
targets of President Reagan's Task Force on Regulatory Relief, chaired
by Vice President Bush. Suspensions or rescissions of these regulations generated an unexpectedly high share of the total regulatory
savings that the task force claimed to have achieved.[8]

Beyond that, state and local government restiveness over mandating can be seen as part and parcel of the attack that economists
launched against regulation in the 1970s. They contended that regulations were arbitrarily enforced, imposed excessive costs and impossible information demands, slowed productivity in both the public
and private sectors, and were generally ineffective. By the 1980s,
early cost studies of the impact of federal regulations on state and
local governments had been completed. These studies not only began
to scale regulatory costs; they demonstrated the often-perverse way
in which costs were distributed with poor jurisdictions often bearing
the largest proportional burdens.

Finally, as David Beam's paper describes, a particularly coercive
and unpopular set of intergovernmental regulatory instruments
emerged in the 1970s. These instruments (which included crosscutting regulations and crossover sanctions) helped catalyze the
mandating debate.

Values and Goals

The mandates issue is intimately bound up with conflict over specific
goals embedded in the social legislation of the 1960s and 1970s.
Dissent over mandates to enforce affirmative action in hiring and
promotions, provide fully accessible transportation to the disabled,
and provide bilingual education paralleled the conflicts these issues
raised elsewhere in society.

Before moving on to a discussion of this volume's major themes, we need to ask: why should direct regulation of state and local governments be treated separately from the problems of federal regulation of the private sector? In brief, the notion of mandating suggests the subjugation of one level of government to a higher level of government. For the states, it can be argued that this demotion defeats constitutional principles of federalism and subverts the limited sovereignty that attaches to states under the Constitution. While these arguments have not proven very influential with the current Supreme Court, their force has waxed and waned over time.[9]

It can also be argued that state and local governments have been induced—or perhaps seduced—into submitting to what appeared to be a partnership with the federal government. Since the 1970s, however, the terms of partnership have changed with the withdrawal of federal support, leaving behind a residue of federal rules and local constituencies for the programs or benefits they mandate. Relations between federal or state regulators and the private sector have not been cloaked in this presumed voluntariness and do not give rise, then, to these equity concerns.

MAJOR THEMES

The following sections of this introduction summarize the major themes presented—definitional issues and issues involved in cost estimation and mandate reimbursement. Each chapter is then summarized.

Definitional Issues

Given the wide range of mandate-related efforts chronicled here, the absence of a common definition of mandate should not be surprising. When the authors' goal is to raise the political consciousness of public officials over the mandating issue, a broad definition is typically adopted. For example, the South Carolina study (chapter 6) defines a mandate as any "situation where a state priority may have been substituted for a local priority."[10] When the state requires a local government to perform a particular service—or to perform it in a particular way—a mandate is imposed. Furthermore, state prohibitions against local use of particular tax instruments are included in South Carolina's inventory of state mandates. Even state requirements that originated as federal requirements imposed on states that have subsequently been passed through to localities are included in the South Carolina definition.

When definitions drive programs and the expenditure of public revenues, mandating tends to be defined more narrowly. Massachusetts, faced with trying to implement a mandate reimbursement program, relies on a very restrictive definition of the term mandate. It includes only regulations imposed after 1980 and excludes court-imposed regulations or federal pass-through rules and regulations.

Issues Involved in Cost Estimation

Estimating the costs that mandates impose on lower-level governments is not only an important component of several mandates studies; it is also frequently proposed to discourage enactment of additional mandates. At the federal level, the Congressional Budget Office (CBO) is required by law to estimate the costs imposed on state and local governments. Forty-two states have similar legislation requiring revenue estimates of the costs imposed on local governments by state laws, resolutions, and administrative actions. These laws are generally known as fiscal note requirements. The major issues surrounding mandate cost estimation are the technical problems of the cost estimation, and the impacts of such estimates on the rate of enactment of new mandates.

Theresa Gullo and Ann Barr describe many of the technical problems that CBO analysts face (chapters 3 and 4) in providing mandate estimates. Their problems include the wide-ranging subject matter of federal legislation, the often vague language of bills, the short time allowed for completing the cost estimates, and the difficulties inherent in estimating costs prior to final congressional action or promulgation of implementing regulations.

The number of lower-level governments affected is likely to make a substantial difference in the difficulty of the cost-estimating process. Anthony D'Aiello, who was more sanguine about the cost-estimating problem in Massachusetts (chapter 9) than were Gullo or Barr about the process at the federal level, noted that Massachusetts used a standard sample of 40 cities and towns to produce estimates for 351 local governments. In comparison, Gullo noted that the Fair Labor Standards Act, one of the most visible recent examples of a federal mandate on state and local governments, was potentially applicable to "7 million public employees in 50 states and approximately 3,000 counties, 19,000 municipalities, 17,000 townships,

15,000 school districts, and 29,000 local special districts. . . ." Similarly, Arnold Kuzmack's description of cost estimation for the Safe Drinking Water Act Amendments of 1986 (chapter 7) noted that 180,000 water systems were affected by the regulations. The greater the number of governmental entities affected by a given regulation, the more difficult the task of estimating mandate costs is likely to be.

The second major issue involving mandate cost estimation is its effectiveness in addressing the mandate problem. There appear to be some conceptual difficulties. One might characterize cost estimation as an effort to make legislators aware of the full costs of their actions. For example, in the absence of mandate cost estimates, Congress might decide on proposed legislation based only on its assessment of benefits and costs to the federal taxpayer. By requiring cost estimates of the impact on lower-level governments, Congress has the opportunity to take into account what are more nearly the full costs.

However, even when Congress becomes aware of the costs to be imposed on lower levels of government, it will not necessarily vote against the legislation being considered. Rational decisionmaking still relies on a comparison of benefits and costs. For any piece of legislation, total benefits may still exceed total costs even when the costs imposed on lower levels of government are taken into account.

For this reason, it is difficult to evaluate Barr's conclusion that "cost estimates had no effect on reducing mandates for five of eight legislative proposals we reviewed at the federal level." This conclusion does not necessarily indicate either the effectiveness or ineffectiveness of cost estimation.

It is also difficult to evaluate the anecdotal information provided by Gullo, Barr, and D'Aiello regarding the use of the cost estimates provided. In most cases at the federal level, it appears that the cost estimates are not an integral part of congressional decisionmaking. In specific instances, such as consideration of the impacts of the Fair Labor Standards Act and the Education of the Handicapped Amendments of 1986, mandate cost estimates appear to have been an important consideration. Yet, it is unclear whether the information provided in cost estimates is more or less useful than many pieces of information used or discarded in one's own decisionmaking, such as the safety records of automobile models. Many consumers do not read *Consumer Reports*, and they ignore government information on the hazards of smoking, but seldom do they maintain that such information is not helpful.

For any policy solution that relies on the provision of information, the information generated will probably be ignored a substantial fraction of the time. The important question is whether, in aggregate, the information provided contributes enough to improved decision-making to warrant the administrative and compliance costs of putting the information together.

An important point regarding the influence of mandate cost estimation is that information alone is not likely to affect decisionmaking. Congress and state legislatures must also have an interest in taking into account the costs they impose on lower-level governments. As James Blum (chapter 11) and Barr point out, interest-group involvement is likely to be key to the usefulness of mandate cost estimates. Or, as Karen Benker put it in her evaluation of state mandate cost estimates, they "provide local governments with powerful lobbying ammunition."[11] Whether local governments or interest groups make use of such ammunition is another matter.

Evaluating the Mandate Reimbursement Option

Mandate reimbursement requires the regulating government to pay all or a share of the compliance costs of the regulated government. So far, 32 states have considered mandate reimbursement legislation and 14 states have adopted it. The mandate reimbursement option has also been proposed at the federal level by Senator Dave Durenberger (R. Minn.) and Congressman Doug Barnard, Jr. (D. Ga.), among others. Congressman Barnard's reimbursement bill (H.R. 1087), for example, would require reimbursement for any mandate imposing more than $25 million in costs on state and local governments as determined by CBO.

According to a General Accounting Office (GAO) study,[12] state reimbursement programs appear not to be relied upon heavily. The reasons include the potential costs of mandate-reimbursement, the administrative costs of implementing a mandate-reimbursement mechanism, and the fear of imposing budgetary inflexibility upon state government.

Although the GAO study (as reported by Richard Horte, chapter 5) concluded that mandate reimbursement has had a greater impact in preventing unfunded mandates than has cost estimation, it also concluded that the overall effectiveness of mandate reimbursement was low. Of seven states with mandate reimbursement that GAO studied intensively, in only four did mandate reimbursement appear to deter unfunded mandates (one state was Massachusetts). On the basis of interviews and survey information in a few states, it appeared that voter-initiated mandate-reimbursement legislation (such as in Massachusetts) appeared to be more effective than legislation originating within the legislature. Furthermore, it appeared that constitutional requirements might be generally more effective than statutory requirements.

As with the evaluation of cost estimation, there are some difficulties in evaluating mandate reimbursement. One conference participant noted that the success of mandate reimbursement cannot be measured by the dollars paid out or by the size of the staff implementing the legislation. The most important question an analyst should ask is: would mandate reimbursement provide greater benefits in improving state legislative action than it imposes in administrative and compliance costs? The evidence appears to be mostly anecdotal, designed to determine whether mandate reimbursement legislation either deterred the state from imposing mandates or forced the state to fund the mandates they impose.

Some indication of the difficulties in determining effectiveness is provided by the debate over the source of funding for the mandates. Sometimes, apparently, states merely earmarked a portion of the funding already allocated for state aid to localities as mandate reimbursement. In such cases, localities are not really being reimbursed for mandates; only the label on the dollar amount of the aid has changed. An even more difficult methodological problem comes to light when one realizes that any mandate reimbursement may come at the expense of increases in state aid to localities that might otherwise have been approved.

SUMMARY OF CHAPTERS

As two of the important early researchers in the mandates area, David Beam and Michael Fix begin this volume.

David Beam describes the origins of the mandates issue within a brief interpretative history of U.S. intergovernmental relations (chapter 1). Beam sets out five stages of federal–state relations, distinguished by their paramount intergovernmental issues. They are, in turn, the constitutional stage from the founding to the 1930s (the era of dual federalism), the political stage from the 1930s to the 1960s (when the doctrine of cooperative federalism took hold), the economic stage of the 1960s, the management stage of the 1970s, and the current stage—regulatory federalism.

Beam notes that federal aid to state and local governments has nearly always been accompanied by program requirements or conditions. He argues that the mandate controversy centers mainly around new types of intergovernmental regulations that are more coercive than the traditional conditions of grants-in-aid. The regulatory requirements of direct orders, crosscutting requirements, crossover sanctions, and partial preemptions cannot be avoided by foregoing particular grant monies. To be exempted from crosscutting requirements, a state or local government can receive no federal aid. Partial preemptions, which establish federal standards for air and water quality, among other examples, can be ignored only if the state-legislated standard exceeds the federal government's.

Beam describes some of the constitutional, political, fiscal, and managerial issues surrounding mandates. For example, he maintains that many federal mandates were enacted without sufficient legislative consideration and that many mandate-based programs are difficult to implement. Beam notes that recent Supreme Court decisions repeal certain constitutional protections against federal mandates and expresses the concern that the federal government may take advantage of this development to enact yet more coercive mandates on state and local governments.

The study by Michael Fix (chapter 2) has a dual purpose: to provide a discussion of the basic issues surrounding mandates that complements Beam's paper and to summarize a 1980 Urban Institute study of the costs selected federal mandates imposed on urban governments.[13] In the conceptual part of his paper, Fix emphasizes the distinction between the policy objectives of federal mandates and the characteristics of the mandate mechanism. He cautions:

While on the one hand, it is inappropriate for a fiscally strapped, deficit-plagued federal government to use its regulatory powers to accomplish objectives that should be achieved via the budget, on the other hand, the federal government should not be held hostage to the states whenever it attempts to accomplish goals of clear national importance.

The Urban Institute's attempt to quantify the costs that six federal mandates imposed on seven urban governments is relevant to the current discussion because there is no recent cost impact research, and because the study raised questions about the appropriate methodology for estimating the costs imposed by mandates and about the appropriate design of any mandate-reimbursement mechanism. The six mandates in question (advanced wastewater treatment requirements, unemployment compensation requirements for state and local employees, bilingual education requirements, the Education of All Handicapped Children Act, transit accessibility requirements, and minimum wage requirements) cost an average of $25 per capita in 1978. The study also found wide variations in impacts across jurisdictions, depending upon such factors as prior level of activity, demographic characteristics, and fiscal conditions. A key finding was that the mandates tended to be regressive, that is, they tended to impose proportionately higher costs on jurisdictions with the lowest fiscal resources.

The chapters by Gullo, Barr, and Horte (chapters 3–5) describe cost estimation and mandate reimbursement and provide a preliminary assessment of their effectiveness.

Gullo (chapter 3) reviews CBO's experience since 1981 in estimating the costs that proposed federal legislation would have on state and local governments. CBO's estimates are required for bills, other than tax or appropriation bills, as they are reported from the full committees of the House and Senate. From 1983 through 1987, CBO prepared state and local cost estimates for 2,800 bills.

Gullo explains that because of the wide diversity of the subject matter of the pending legislation affecting state and local governments, CBO has not been able to set up a routine methodology, database or network for computing cost estimates. The required estimates at the legislative stage mean that the analysts must make cost projections without knowing how the relevant regulatory agency will implement the final legislation. At the same time that the office is challenged by mammoth information requirements, it often has little time (sometimes only a few days) after the bill is reported from committee to produce the cost estimate. Despite the difficulties of the task and CBO's perception that Congress generally has only a limited interest in its estimates, Gullo concludes that on balance the State and Local Cost Estimate Act makes a positive contribution to intergovernmental relations and to the rationality of federal legislation.

Barr (chapter 4) goes beyond discussion of the mandate cost estimation process at the federal level to consider the cost estimation procedures used in 42 states. She summarizes and interprets findings from a recent GAO report[14] that evaluated state and federal cost estimation procedures, using the state experience to suggest federal mandate cost estimation improvements.

Barr presents three recommendations for improving the federal mandate cost estimation process: estimates could be made before bills are cleared by the committees with the hope that information made available earlier would have a greater impact on legislation, estimates could be updated as proposed legislation is amended, and cost estimates could be provided for all types of bills, including appropriation and tax bills. She also suggests that current CBO information could be used to prepare periodic reports on the total cost of mandates imposed by federal legislation and that increased state and local public-interest group involvement would motivate Congress to pay more attention to the CBO mandate cost estimates.

Although cost estimation is frequently used, mandate reimbursement, which requires a government to pay for the costs it imposes on lower level governments, is a more stringent and less used remedy. Horte (chapter 5) reports that 32 states have formally considered the mandate-reimbursement option, but only 14 have adopted such a requirement.

According to Horte, if reimbursement is effective, one of three results should be observable: mandate reimbursement should be paid, fewer mandates should be imposed, or legislation should be altered to reduce the burden of mandates. The GAO study of mandate reimbursement, which Horte summarized, found that, to the extent that mandate reimbursement was effective, its primary effect was in deterring the passage of mandates. GAO classified four of its seven case study states as having a reimbursement process with a significant impact in deterring mandates.

The GAO study found that mandate reimbursement had a greater impact in preventing the enactment of unfunded mandates than did cost estimation; even so, the effectiveness of mandate reimbursement was relatively low. Horte lists several ways in which a state can satisfy the letter of the mandate reimbursement law but still enact unfunded mandates. For example, state legislation may define a mandate narrowly. Or it may provide no up-front funding of mandates; then local governments must accept imposed costs until they secure a favorable determination from the courts. Based on state experience, Horte does not recommend federal adoption of a mandate-reimbursement procedure. Instead, he recommends a strategy of increasing state and local interest group involvement or of providing periodic reports on the cumulative impact of federal mandates.

Janet Kelly's is the first of several case or state studies included here (chapter 6). She reports the results of an 18-month effort by the South Carolina Advisory Commission on Intergovernmental Relations to examine the mandates problem as viewed by the cities and towns. The main conclusion of the study was that the mandate problem in South Carolina is the cumulative impact of the 649 state mandates on local governments. The problem is not one of poorly crafted or especially expensive mandates but the cumulative effect on local finances and operations of them all.

Kelly notes that a large proportion of state mandates on local governments in South Carolina restricts the day-to-day operations of those governments by regulating administrative matters such as record-keeping or fee-levying. State aid to local governments does not adequately compensate for the mandate burden, and the burden of unfunded mandates falls disproportionately on the poorest jurisdictions. One recommendation made is that South Carolina comply with the present mandate cost-estimation law. To date, it has had no effect on deterring the passage of mandates simply because no mandate cost estimates have been made.

The second case study (chapter 7), by Kuzmack, is of a particular federal mandate from the point of view of an EPA official responsible for its implementation. His is an interim report on implementation of the Safe Drinking Water Act Amendments of 1986. They require EPA to set standards for many water contaminants—83 in the next three years, then for 25 additional contaminants every three years, indefinitely. At one level, this mandate represents a partial preemption of state authority as administration of the federal standard is delegated to the states. At another level, it functions as a direct order because local governments that provide drinking water must meet federal standards.

Kuzmack focuses on EPA estimates of the costs this mandate is expected to impose on the more than 180,000 public water systems in the United States, on the difficulties involved in implementing the mandate, and on the strategies EPA is using to alleviate these difficulties. EPA estimates the current state cost of complying with this mandate at $1 to 2 billion per year, a reduction from the $3 billion per year originally estimated by CBO and EPA.

EPA's aim in implementing the mandate is to minimize compliance costs for state and local governments and water systems without compromising targeted gains in water quality. To achieve its goal, EPA is working with interest groups to inform them of the requirements and is encouraging states to seek innovative approaches to implementing the standards or funding compliance costs. From his vantage point in helping to implement this particular federal mandate, Kuzmack argues that, assuming that it is in the interests of the people to improve water quality standards and given that the U.S. taxpayer will ultimately pay for this improvement no matter the funding mechanism, it does not necessarily follow that these costs should be paid from the federal budget. In other words, Kuzmack questions the blanket presumption against enactment of unfunded federal mandates.

The chapters by Emily Lunceford and D'Aiello (chapters 8 and 9) present a detailed description of the mandate reimbursement statute, cost estimation, and reimbursement process in Massachusetts, one of the four states Horte describes as having an effective mandate reimbursement program.

The Massachusetts mandate statute was enacted in 1980 as a citizens' initiative. It was part of the taxpayers' revolt that resulted in one of the most stringent property tax limitations in the country, Proposition 2½. It was thought that without mandate reimbursement, the stringent property tax limits in combination with state-mandated services might bankrupt certain cities and towns. For many years after enactment of Proposition 2½ and mandate reimbursement, the Massachusetts economy was booming (the Massachusetts miracle touted in Governor Dukakis's campaign for the presidency), enabling the state to afford increasing aid to cities and towns as well as mandate reimbursement. Only recently have tax revenues slowed. The state is now facing a budget crisis and is likely soon to face the first true test of its commitment to both the property tax limit and mandate-reimbursement statutes.

Lunceford describes the Massachusetts legislative definition of a mandate in her discussion of the steps the Division of Local Mandates takes to determine whether proposed or enacted state legislation imposes a mandate. As noted above, the Massachusetts definition of mandates is rather narrow. The law does not provide reimbursement for mandates enacted before 1981; for court-imposed mandates, federally imposed mandates, mandates on school districts or regional governments; or for laws regulating the benefits of municipal employment. Furthermore, reimbursement is not required if the city or town has the option of not complying with the mandate, even if the option might not be a realistic one, such as when a locality might have to forego a substantial amount of state aid in order to avoid the mandate.

According to D'Aiello (chapter 9), the Division of Local Mandates (DLM) prefers to see mandates funded on an up-front basis, and to that end, it tracks about 6,000 bills annually to detect impending unfunded mandates. Survey instruments are sent to a sample of cities and towns, and a computer model is used to estimate the cost of a pending mandate. The legislative unit of DLM provides this information to legislative committees with the hope that legislators will provide up-front funding for the mandate. This process has worked in a number of instances cited by D'Aiello. For example, a 1983 bill requiring extended polling hours resulted in $3 million in up-front funds for local governments to compensate them for increased election costs.

Nevertheless, unfunded mandates are sometimes enacted. Then DLM is responsible for obtaining documentation for costs imposed on cities and towns to implement the reimbursement process. Since establishment of DLM in 1983, $20 million in state funding has been provided to Massachusetts cities and towns for mandate reimbursement.

The last case study, by Geary Maher (chapter 10) is Connecticut's, whose experience on the mandates issue differs from that of Massachusetts. When unfunded mandates became an issue in Connecticut about six years ago, a mandate-reimbursement program was considered and rejected. After studying the issue, the legislature provided for voluntary mandate reimbursement. Bills imposing mandates are to be referred to the Appropriations Committee, which, in turn, determines whether a mandate is being imposed and whether and how costs would be reimbursed when it reports the bill. No direct reimbursement has been provided through this legislation. The state has increased its funding of local property tax relief grants since the mandates issue became prominent, thus indirectly alleviating the pressure for mandate reimbursement. Maher summarizes the Connecticut mandates experience with the tongue-in-cheek title, "the rise and fall of the reimbursement issue in the land of steady habits."

The last chapter presents general policy conclusions and recommendations. Blum (chapter 11) discusses the mandates issue and alternatives to mandates reimbursement from the CBO perspective. Blum divides proposals to focus attention on the costs imposed by federal mandates before such mandates are enacted into three types: proposals for improving the flow of information, proposals for improving the use of such information on the part of state and local interest groups, and proposals for altering the federal legislative process by, for example, requiring either up-front funding of mandates or mandate reimbursement.

Of his three alternatives, Blum clearly favors more aggressive intervention by state and local interest groups in the legislative process using available information. He argues that placing greater informational demands on CBO, for example, by requiring cost estimates for more types of bills or for amended bills, as Barr suggests, is likely to be ineffective given the limited current demand for information on mandates costs. Blum is also critical of imposing a federal mandate reimbursement requirement or a point-of-order option, especially if CBO cost estimates would be critical to this political process. He is concerned about the workability of either option, especially in the light of continued large federal budget deficits.

CONCLUDING OBSERVATIONS

With few exceptions, discussions of mandating are dominated by the protests of those who are interested in limiting or eliminating intergovernmental regulations. The perspectives of the beneficiaries of mandates (e.g., the disabled) or of the regulating government are less frequently brought to bear. As a result, these discussions have often failed to: (1) reflect adequately the claims to legitimacy accorded to different mandates, (2) disaggregate the differing types of impacts that individual mandates generate, and (3) reach the complex implementation issues raised by mandates.

Legitimacy

Too often, it seems, mandates are classed as a homogeneous bad that belies their varying claims to legitimacy. It can be argued that federal and state governments can appropriately impose certain types of mandates, even when these mandates are not funded. For example, one set of mandates serves to protect the rights of political minorities that might not otherwise be upheld by local political processes. In other instances, mandates force state and local governments to internalize the costs of spillovers that would otherwise be borne by other jurisdictions (e.g., regulations forcing upstream polluters to treat their own wastes).

But, these claims for legitimacy are far weaker when, for example, mandates force jurisdictions to set environmental standards higher than they otherwise would and no spillover effects occur. In such instances, virtue may be its own reward and, arguably, the decision to be virtuous (i.e., treat wastes) could rest with the political jurisdiction and its electorate. Similarly, mandates that impose onerous accountability standards and high compliance costs that represent a waste of resources have weak legitimacy claims.

Differing Impacts

Little is known about the distribution of mandates' costs across differing types of jurisdictions and, thus, what their implications might be for both legitimacy and reimbursement. For example, some types of mandates may impose disproportionate costs on certain types of political units—on special districts, towns, counties, cities, or states. Because cities and counties have lost far more in federal intergovernmental transfers over the course of the past decade than have states, the relative burden that mandates impose on local jurisdictions may be both greater and, in some sense, less equitable than that imposed on states.

Further, the little research completed on impacts to date indicates that mandates tend to have a regressive impact, imposing the highest costs on those jurisdictions that are least able to pay.[15] For example, the burden of paying unemployment compensation to public workers tends to fall most heavily on the poorest jurisdictions because they tend to be hardest hit by economic downturns and the layoffs that result. As Kuzmack states (chapter 7), mandates, like all regulatory regimes, are likely to have scale effects. As a result, smaller jurisdictions tend to be disproportionately disadvantaged by regulations such as those promulgated under the Safe Drinking Water Act that require even minimal capital investments.

Implementation Issues

In October 1987, President Reagan signed Executive Order 12612, which requires, among other things, that principles of federalism guide "the executive departments and agencies in the formulation and implementation of policies."[16] If federal agencies attempt to implement the order, they will need to examine the federalism implications of virtually the whole range of their governmental activities.[17] This activity would require not only an examination of whether a proposed action falls within the constitutional powers of the federal government but a systematic inquiry into how a series of mandate-related implementation issues is addressed. Such an investigation would include:

☐ the timing and character of notice given to state and local governments of federal activity,
☐ the administrative discretion granted states in complying with federal mandates,

☐ the deference to be granted the states in standard setting,
☐ the use of regulations that preempt state authority, and
☐ the degree to which conditions of aid must be related directly to the purpose of the grant.

The principal instrument to be used to achieve these purposes will be the preparation of a federalism assessment whenever a proposed action has sufficient (but otherwise unenumerated) federalism implications. Whether the order is vigorously implemented or whether it remains a symbolic gesture has yet to be demonstrated.

One of the least examined implementation issues is the quality of the monitoring and enforcement strategies that regulating governments use to ensure compliance with mandates. Ideally, such strategies would reinforce state or national policy objectives without being unduly intrusive. In point of fact, unspoken issues in the mandates discussion are the limited monitoring that occurs and the reluctance of regulating governments to penalize noncompliant jurisdictions. What weak enforcement has meant for compliance and for the credibility of the underlying regulatory regimes is not known.

In sum, in the design of strategies to deal with mandates, future discussions of alternative strategies that move beyond the perspectives presented in this volume should take care to: (1) distinguish between the legitimate and illegitimate use of intergovernmental regulation, viewing those regulations not just through the eye of the regulated entity but also that of the regulating government and the target population; (2) identify and account for variation in the impacts of differing regulations across jurisdictions, factoring in such concerns as type of legal entity, size, and fiscal and demographic characteristics; and (3) examine such critical implementation issues as the effectiveness and intrusiveness of the monitoring and enforcement strategies adopted by the regulating government.

Notes

1. U.S. Government Printing Office, Washington, D.C.: 1984.

2. See, for example, "Mandates without Money," National Journal, 4 October 1986.

3. This taxonomy of intergovernmental regulations is drawn from Regulatory Federalism, pp. 1–16.

4. W. F. Pedersen, Jr., "Federal/State Relations in the Clean Air Act, the Clean Water

Act, and RCRA: Does the Pattern Make Sense?" *Environmental Law Reporter*, 12(1983): 15069.

5. Ibid.

6. Garcia v. San Antonio Metropolitan Transit Authority, 105 S. Ct. 1005 (1985).

7. But as Jerry Mashaw and Susan Rose-Ackerman point out, at the same time, mandates can prove valuable even to politicians and officials within regulated governments. These officials may need the political "cover" of mandates to govern responsibly in the face of powerful, entrenched local interests. In these cases, the mandate permits officials to shift the blame for enforcing certain standards or distributing benefits to certain groups to those federal or state officials over whom they have no control. See J. L. Mashaw and S. Rose-Ackerman, "Federalism and Regulation," in *The Reagan Regulatory Strategy, An Assessment*, G. Eads and M. Fix, eds. (Washington, D.C.: Urban Institute Press, 1984).

8. See, for example, "Presidential Task Force on Regulatory Relief, Reagan Administration Achievements in Regulatory Relief, A Progress Report," (Washington, D.C., August 1982). Although regulatory federalism remained a theme of the Reagan administration, in retrospect, its regulatory relief objectives were only partially realized. The reasons were political conflict over the administration's early regulatory efforts and its own willingness to invoke intergovernmental regulations to achieve other conflicting political objectives such as the elimination of waste, fraud, and abuse. See, generally, T. Conlan, *New Federalism, Intergovernmental Reform from Nixon to Reagan* (Washington, D.C.: Brookings Institution, 1988).

9. See, for example, the relatively expansive reading of the Tenth Amendment of the Constitution in National League of Cities v. Usery declaring unconstitutional congressional extension of the Fair Labor Standards Act to the majority of state and local employees. The Court found that the extension violated the Tenth Amendment by "directly displacing the states' freedom to structure integral operations in areas of traditional governmental functions." 426 U.S. 852 (1976). The decision's constitutional foundation, the Tenth Amendment, holds, "The powers not delegated to the United States by the Constitution, nor prohibited by it to the states, are reserved to the states respectively, or to the people."

10. Janet M. Kelly, *State Mandated Local Government Expenditures and Revenue Limitations in South Carolina* (Columbia: South Carolina Advisory Commission on Intergovernmental Relations: 1988).

11. Karen Benker, "More State Budget and Tax Management Tools" (draft report for the Advisory Commission on Intergovernmental Relations, 12 September 1984).

12. *Legislative Mandates: State Experiences Offer Insights for Federal Action* (Washington, D.C.: General Accounting Office, 1988).

13. Thomas Muller and Michael Fix, "The Impact of Selected Federal Actions on Municipal Outlays," in U.S. Congress, Joint Economic Committee, Special Study on Economic Change, Vol. 5 *Government Regulation: Achieving Social and Economic Balance* (Washington, D.C.: U.S. Government Printing Office, 1980).

14. *Legislative Mandates.*

15. Cf. Muller and Fix, note 11, supra; chapter 6.

16. E.O. 12612, 26 October 1987 states, in part, that it is "intended to restore the division of governmental responsibilities between the national government and the States that was intended by the Framers of the Constitution and to ensure that the

principles of federalism established by the Framers guide the Executive departments and agencies in the formulation and implementation of policies."

17. Section 1 (a) of E.O. 12612 states: "Policies that have federalism implications" refer to "regulations, legislative comments or proposed legislation, and other policy statements or actions that have substantial direct effects on the States, on the relationship between the national government and the States, or on the distribution of power and responsibilities among the various levels of government."

Chapter One

ON THE ORIGINS OF THE MANDATE ISSUE

David R. Beam

The character of the dialogue about intergovernmental relations with the United States changed markedly in the late 1970s and early 1980s. To many public officials, and to many observers, the reign of what had traditionally been termed cooperative federalism seemed to be at an end. Other "c" words—like compulsory, coercive, and conflictual—were suggested to describe patterns of federal–state–local relationships that centered not on well-established financial grants-in-aid programs but on disputes over new kinds of federal rules and regulations.

Although public officials often complained loudly about the costs of these unfunded mandates, as they were frequently described, in fact, the issue raised was not solely, and perhaps not even chiefly, fiscal. There were coequal concerns about *status*—the pointed lack of respect for the position of states and localities as constitutional entities within the federal system. Cities and states feared that they were becoming the "field hands of federalism"—simply, tools for implementing national policy directives in environmental protection, race, sex and age nondiscrimination, handicapped access and education, bilingual education, health planning, and other areas. They did not welcome a diminution in their roles, regardless of the wages paid.

Other issues were raised: doubts about the effectiveness of program implementation—whether the new regulatory devices could achieve their goals—and how realistic were the objectives that had been set.

In sum, the mandating question, as it took form at the beginning of this decade, was no simple or single issue, at least not to state and local officials and other partisans of a balanced federalism. Instead, it reflected a whole range of concerns related to the growth of a complex, challenging, and in many ways troubled system of legal, fiscal, administrative, and political relations that merited a new name: regulatory federalism.[1]

THE RISE OF REGULATORY FEDERALISM

A review of history suggests that intergovernmental relations (IGR) have moved through a number of phases or stages, with the rate of change accelerating in recent decades along with the growth of national domestic programs. Although interpretations vary, intergovernmental mandating is best put into perspective by viewing this history in five segments, each of which brought a different face of IGR to public attention. Regulatory federalism is the most recent phase.

From the nation's founding to the 1930s, federal–state relations were viewed primarily as a *constitutional* question of determining which powers were delegated to Congress and which were reserved to the states. This period was the regime of dual federalism, which lasted until the New Deal, when expansive interpretations of national authority under the commerce and spending powers became accepted judicial doctrine. Thereafter, subnational governments lacked a clear sphere of responsibility protected by the nation's fundamental law, though shields of other kinds remained.

From the 1930s to the 1960s, the question of federal–state roles came to be viewed in *political* terms. The problem was no longer one of determining what initiatives would be accepted by the courts; it was seeing which proposals for new national action Congress could adopt. Battles between liberal Democrats and the conservative coalition of Republicans and Southern Democrats typified the era. Then, too, the doctrine of cooperative federalism took hold among both scholars and thoughtful public leaders.[2] In emphasizing the historic elements of "sharing" public functions and mixed federal–state–local responsibilities for determining policy and administering public services, this new view also rationalized or legitimized the growth of national grants in a host of fields, quieting objections about possible overcentralization.

As the political obstacles to national action melted away during the mid-1960s, there was a tendency to view IGR *economically*, as a method of achieving a more technically efficient allocation of resources among levels of government. The national government at the time clearly possessed a much stronger and more progressive tax base, and the concept of externalities presented a theoretical rationale for new assistance programs in many traditional spheres of state and local responsibility, including education.

With so many new programs operating during the Great Society years, problems of *management* were immediately dominant. Often disappointing program results were published; other reports traced the difficulties of program implementation. This was the era in which policy efforts were directed toward grant coordination, grant consolidation, and general revenue sharing. In addition, during the 1970s, both Presidents Nixon and Carter launched parallel drives to reorganize and improve the management of the federal executive branch.

In the late 1970s and into the 1980s, issues of *regulation* became the focal point for intergovernmental observers. In this, a fifth stage in the development of U.S. federalism, state and local officials vocally protested programmatic requirements that they viewed as inflexible, inefficient, ill-considered, intrusive, and expensive. New York Mayor Edward I. Koch challenged the wisdom of Washington's "mandate mandarins," who offered sweeping, costly, and sometimes untested solutions to local problems.[3] He urged remedies like waivers, alternative methods of compliance, and the provision of adequate aid to achieve stipulated goals. Researchers, too, struggled to define and measure the underlying problem and identify root causes of the new intergovernmental tension. Key contributions to the mandate literature included studies by Catherine Lovell, beginning in 1979;[4] Thomas Muller and Michael Fix's work in 1980;[5] and the report of the Advisory Commission of Intergovernmental Relations (ACIR), *Regulatory Federalism: Policy, Progress, Impact and Reform*,[6] with findings and recommendations completed in 1982.

A host of other studies examined particular programs. One assessment of the 1970 Clean Air Act Amendments pointed out crucial differences between current policies and their predecessors in these terms:

Whereas past policy reflected a sort of "cooperative federalism" consisting in some national but also considerable state authority, that of the present underscores "federal" and is distinctly . . . uncooperative. Pollution policy is national policy, and the states are little more than reluctant minions mandated to do the dirty work—to implement federal directives often distasteful at the local level . . . .The fact that federal policy of today is simply the culmination of a slow but steady trend that began years ago should not obscure the essential difference between old policy and new, between federalism and federalization.[7]

THE NATURE OF THE MANDATE PROBLEM

Why did this new awareness of mandate burdens appear in the late 1970s? Four factors seem to have been involved:

□ The major programs of "new social regulation"[8] adopted in the 1960s and 1970s—particularly nondiscrimination and environmental protection policies—were coming on line by 1980. For the first time, their full and combined force was being felt. With a single exception, all the mandates identified as "most burdensome" to state and local governments by impact studies came from this group.[9]

□ Federal aid growth had slowed after 1978; at the same time there was also a tax revolt in many states. State and local officials were poignantly aware of the cost burdens imposed on them by various federal standards and requirements.

□ There was a mounting expert consensus against governmental regulation in general. A movement to deregulate transportation and many other fields paralleled concern with intergovernmental mandating.

□ The public mood was important. The late 1970s was an era of general concern about bloated and overbearing government, resulting in the election of Jimmy Carter in 1976 and then Ronald Reagan in 1980.

What most deserves emphasis, however, is the fact that state and local officials had correctly identified new kinds of programmatic pressures emanating from Washington, sharply changing the character of the old intergovernmental partnership. With the exception of general revenue sharing, federal assistance programs had always come with strings attached, that is, grants were conditional. Although objections could be, and were often, voiced by mayors and governors about excessive red tape and duplicative, contradictory, or otherwise onerous program requirements, such conditions of aid gained legitimacy from the fact that acceptance of the grants to which they were attached was clearly voluntary. To accept federal funds was to agree to be bound by certain national standards and rules.

In contrast, the new programs of intergovernmental regulation that were the principal focus of the mandate controversy were much more obligatory. Unlike previous requirements, they could not be avoided by the simple expedient of not accepting a particular narrowly defined categorical grant, and, in some cases, they could not be avoided at all. These program types (paralleling the commonly recognized classification of grants as formula and project categoricals, block grants, and revenue sharing) were defined in the ACIR study:[10]

Direct orders—the fewest but most intrusive—which mandated state or local actions under the threat of criminal or civil penalties, with the Fair Labor Standards Act Amendments of 1974, which applied federal minimum wage and overtime pay provisions to state and local government employees, as an example.

Crosscutting requirements—applied to all or many federal assistance programs, as with the Davis–Bacon Act, Title IX of the 1972 Education Amendments (sex discrimination), or the National Environmental Policy Act's environmental impact statement process. For example, the Davis–Bacon Act required that the "prevailing wage" be paid to construction workers employed under federal aid programs.

Crossover sanctions that threatened the termination or reduction of aid provided under one or more specified programs unless the requirements of another program are satisfied, as found in the Education for All Handicapped Children Act and Highway Beautification Act. Under the latter, failure to comply with federal outdoor advertising standards on major roads can result in the loss of some highway construction grant funds.

Partial preemptions establishing federal standards but delegating administration to the states if they establish standards equivalent to the national ones. This system is found in the Clean Air, Clean Water, and Safe Drinking Water Acts, as well as in other environmental programs and the Occupational Safety and Health Act (OSHA).

In all, 34 statutes in these four categories were enacted between 1960 and 1980, as table 1.1 shows, with more than half enacted after 1972.

THE FOUR FACES OF THE MANDATE ISSUE

These new intergovernmental regulatory programs also raised, in a somewhat altered guise, issues from the four phases or faces of intergovernmental relations of prior times. That is, they provoked new legal, political, fiscal, and administrative concerns, each requiring attention.

The legal or *constitutional* face reasserted itself, most notably with the *National League of Cities v. Usery* decision in 1976, which seemed for a time to reestablish a constitutionally protected sphere of autonomous state action. As in the 1930s, the courts became an important arena of intergovernmental activity, and legal challenges were mounted by state and local governments against many of the new federal regulatory programs. These efforts were bolstered by the creation of the State and Local Legal Center in 1982.

The *political* considerations involved in mandating were also quite important. Legislative histories show that many federal intergovernmental mandates were ill-considered by Congress at their time of

Table 1.1 MAJOR STATUTES OF INTERGOVERNMENTAL REGULATION,
         1960–80

1964 Civil Rights Act (Title VI)	1973 Flood Disaster Protection Act
1965 Highway Beautification Act	Rehabilitation Act (Section 504)
Water Quality Act	Endangered Species Act
1966 National Historic Preservation Act	1974 Age Discrimination Employment Act
1967 Wholesome Meat Act	Safe Drinking Water Act
	National Health Planning and Resources Development Act
1968 Civil Rights Act (Title VIII)	
Architectural Barriers Act	Emergency Highway Energy Conservation Act
Wholesome Poultry Products Act	
1969 National Environmental Policy Act	Family Educational Rights and Privacy Act
1970 Occupational Safety and Health Act	Fair Labor Standards Act Amendments
Clear Air Act Amendments	1975 Education for All Handicapped Children Act
Uniform Relocation Assistance and Real Property Acquisition Policies Act	Age Discrimination Act
	1976 Resource Conservation and Recovery Act
1972 Federal Water Pollution Control Act Amendments	1977 Surface Mining Control and Reclamation Act
Equal Employment Opportunity Act	Marine Protection Research and Sanctuaries Act Amendments
Education Act Amendments (Title IX)	1978 National Energy Conservation Policy Act
Coastal Zone Management Act	Public Utility Regulatory Policy Act
Federal Insecticide, Fungicide, and Rodenticide Act	Natural Gas Policy Act

Source: Advisory Commission on Intergovernmental Relations, *Regulatory Federalism: Policy, Process, Impact and Reform* (Washington, D.C.: U.S. Government Printing Office, 1984), p. 6.

enactment. Because they addressed objectives of environmental quality or civil rights viewed by some as of overarching importance, such legislation was often treated more as a symbol of commitment than a substantive operating program.[11] The fact that the new regulatory programs were partly cost-free to the national government encouraged this same sort of cursory scrutiny and design.

Fiscally, mandating raised the question of who should pay. Although no accurate total could be developed, it is clear that some mandates impose substantial costs on at least some state and local governments. Federal aid programs created to help meet these costs in some program areas are often underfunded. Mechanisms to ensure full or partial reimbursement of mandated costs, along with improved cost estimation procedures, were among the proposed solutions.

The *administrative* record suggests that many mandate-based programs are also hard to implement. They often had lofty, unrealistic policy goals, took very long to write rules for and launch successfully, were troubled by conflict during the implementation phase, were marked by an inability or unwillingness of federal agencies to impose specified sanctions, and faced repeated extensions of time limits and statutory deadlines.[12] Thus, it is by no means clear that federal mandates—tougher though they sound—represent a more effective means of accomplishing national policy objectives than the voluntary grant programs they had replaced or augmented.

CONCLUSION

This historical account provides a background for considering the mandate issue. The studies cited earlier, together with mounting protests from mayors, governors, and other officials, created a new IGR policy agenda at the beginning of the decade. It was partly addressed by the administration, Senator Dave Durenberger, and other congressional leaders over the eight years of the Reagan presidency.[13]

Yet, despite drives for regulatory relief and intergovernmental decentralization, intergovernmental mandating remains a leading concern of state and local officials. A recent report of the National Governor's Association suggests a host of proposals for legislative and administrative consideration while charging that "the federal government unnecessarily micro-manages many issues, programs, and projects in the states."[14] Similarly, a document prepared by the National League of Cities for discussion by presidential contenders during the 1988 campaign shows the nature of the mayoral view. Its section on "partnerships with local government" stresses the obstacles created by federal mandates and federal preemption *first*—and only secondarily and much more briefly—comments on trends in federal financial aid.[15] This is a dramatic change from the way intergovernmental matters were viewed a decade or two ago, when grants-in-aid issues always had priority.

The most vociferous protests could be ahead. The record of recent decades suggests that federal policymakers are inclined to turn to mandates at times when fiscal resources are scarce, as they are now, given deficit pressures. At the same time, the Supreme Court's decisions in *Garcia v. San Antonio Metropolitan Transit Authority*[16] (1985) and in *South Carolina v. Baker*[17] (1988) make it clear that states and localities cannot expect any Tenth Amendment protection against federal regulatory intrusion.[18] What remains uncertain is whether Congress, the Bush administration, or its successors will move through the door that the judiciary has opened wide, making the often protested federal mandates of the 1960s and 1970s seem no more than weak predecessors of others yet to come.

Notes

1. This term is taken from a study by the Advisory Commission on Intergovernmental Relations, *Regulatory Federalism: Policy, Process, Impact and Reform* (Washington, D.C.: U.S. Government Printing Office, 1984), directed by the author of this chapter.

2. A classic statement of this position is presented by Morton Grodyins in his essay, "The Federal System," in President's Commission on National Goals, *Goals for Americans* (New York: Prentice-Hall, Inc., 1960), pp. 265 ff.

3. Edward I. Koch, "The Mandate Millstone," *Public Interest* 61 (Fall 1980).

4. Catherine H. Lovell et al., *Federal and State Mandating on Local Governments: An Exploration of Issues* (Riverside, Calif.: Graduate School of Administration, University of California, Riverside, 1979).

5. Thomas Muller and Michael Fix, "The Impact of Selected Federal Actions on Municipal Outlays," in U.S. Congress, Joint Economic Committee *Special Study on Economic Change*, vol. 5, *Government Regulation: Achieving Social and Economic Balance*, (Washington, D.C.: U.S. Government Printing Office, 1980), pp. 326–77. An abbreviated version appeared in Thomas Muller and Michael Fix, "Federal Solicitude, Local Costs: The Impact of Federal Regulation on Municipal Finances," *Regulation* (July/August 1980): 29–36.

6. Washington, D.C.: U.S. Government Printing Office, 1984.

7. James A. Krier and Edmund Ursin, *Pollution and Policy* (Berkeley, Calif.: University of California Press, 1977), pp. 297–98.

8. This term seems to have originated with William Lilley, III and James C. Miller, III, "The New 'Social Regulation'," *Public Interest* 47 (Spring 1977): 49–61. It is used conventionally to distinguish health, safety, environmental, and nondiscrimination regulations from traditional economic regulation concerned with rates, entry, and condition of service in particular industries. See George C. Eads and Michael Fix, *Relief or Reform?: Reagan's Regulation Dilemma* (Washington, D.C.: The Urban Institute, 1984), pp. 12–15.

9. See *Regulatory Federalism*, p. 184. The exception was the Davis–Bacon Act of 1931.

10. Regulatory Federalism, pp. 7–10.

11. See Timothy J. Conlan and Steven L. Abrams, "Federal Intergovernmental Regulation: Symbolic Politics in the New Congress," *Intergovernmental Perspective* 7 (Summer 1981): 19–26.

12. See David R. Beam, "From Law to Rule: Exploring the Maze of Intergovernmental Regulation," *Intergovernmental Perspective* 9 (Spring 1983): 7–22.

13. For discussion of the Reagan administration's intergovernmental regulatory relief initiatives, see Marshall R. Goodman and Margaret T. Wrightson, *Managing Regulation Reform* (New York: Praeger, 1987), and George C. Eads and Michael Fix, eds., *The Reagan Regulatory Strategy: An Assessment* (Washington, D.C.: The Urban Institute, 1984).

14. National Governor's Association, *Regulatory Reform Initiative: Restoring the Balance: State Leadership for America's Future* (Washington, D.C.: National Governor's Association, 1988), p. 2.

15. National League of Cities Institute, *Investing in Home Town America: Ten Issues of the 1988 Elections* (Washington, D.C.: National League of Cities Institute, 1988).

16. Garcia v. San Antonio Metropolitan Transit Authority, 105 S.Ct. 1005(1985).

17. South Carolina v. Baker, Treasury Secretary of the United States, 485 U.S., 99 L. Ed. 2d 592, 108 S.Ct.

18. See Margaret T. Wrightson, "The Road to South Carolina: Intergovernmental Tax Immunity and the Constitutional Status of Federalism," *Publius* 19 (Summer 1989): 39–55.

Chapter Two

OBSERVATIONS ON MANDATING

Michael Fix

This brief presentation has two objectives: first, to set out several problems behind the mandates label and to suggest that analysts balance the policy objectives achieved through mandates with the problems created by the mandating mechanism; second, to summarize some of the early work on what is referred to in other chapters as the mandating problem. The study discussed here was done for the Joint Economic Committee of the Congress almost 10 years ago.[1] It attempted to quantify the costs of six federal mandates for seven urban jurisdictions, and it raised many of the methodological issues confronting efforts to estimate regulatory costs and develop equitable reimbursement schemes.

MANDATING: DIFFERENT ISSUES, DIFFERENT SOLUTIONS, VARYING PROGRESS

The mandating problem is really a number of problems. Put perhaps too simplistically, the root issues reduce to legitimacy and money.

The legitimacy issue goes to the very right of the federal government to override state sovereignty and dictate to the states. The reach of this Tenth Amendment-based state sovereignty argument—so tantalizingly embraced in *NLC v. Usery*,[2] has subsequently been eviscerated by a series of Supreme Court decisions, most notably, *Garcia v. San Antonio Metropolitan Transit Authority*.[3] Given the concern for states rights over the past decade, it seems ironic that the power of state sovereignty as a legal argument should now seem so weak as a defense against the mandating problem.

At another level, the legitimacy of federal mandates has less to do with the right of the federal government to dictate to state and local governments than with the latitude provided state and local governments to meet federal requirements. In this case, the issue is one of regulatory reform: permitting state and local governments the freedom to respond to federal standards in a manner that reflects local economic, physical, and other realities. This goal has been achieved in recent years through the introduction of such devices as the substitution of performance for design standards and the use of market-based regulatory mechanisms such as emissions trading.

The legitimacy of federal mandates also goes to what might be termed institutional due process—to the rights of states and local governments to be more deeply involved in shaping regulatory standards and to providing and receiving accurate information about the impact of proposed efforts. The solution here is increased consultation and exploitation of such notice devices as fiscal notes. Based on other chapters in this volume, this is one policy area in which substantial progress has been made over the past decade.

If federal intergovernmental regulation—mandating—has some measure of legitimacy, then it seems the real issue is one of money. The cost problem can be attacked two ways. The first and most obvious solution is reimbursement, the subject of several other chapters here. The second way to attack regulatory costs is, again, through regulatory reform: by diminishing the costs associated with the regulatory process and permitting state and local governments more freedom to devise their own strategies for achieving regulatory standards.

In the final analysis, then, solutions to the mandating problem should go beyond the cost-estimation and reimbursement issues.

THE PROBLEM WITH THE MANDATE PROBLEM

When this issue last emerged—during the late 1970s and the early 1980s—the mandating discussion provided an extremely useful catalyst for a long overdue reevaluation of the proper balance of fiscal and governmental responsibilities within the federal system. However, this rather careful federalism discussion was later distorted to serve the regulation-bashing objectives of many who had grown impatient with a rise in the size and power of the federal government.

This point is made to urge that we do not lose sight of the fact that, but for these problem mandates, we would have far lower rates of progress in providing education to the handicapped and public transportation to disadvantaged populations, in cleaning up drinking-water supplies, and in achieving other important *national* goals on which there is a wide consensus. The power of these objectives tends to get lost in discussions of the mandating mechanism. While on the one hand, it is not appropriate for a fiscally strapped, deficit-plagued federal government to use its regulatory powers to accomplish objectives that should be achieved via the budget, on the other hand, the federal government should not be held hostage to the states whenever it attempts to accomplish goals of clear national importance.

THE COSTS OF FEDERAL MANDATES: AN EARLY ASSESSMENT

Although The Urban Institute's 1979 study[4] is clearly outdated, it provides some useful historical perspective on this issue while speaking of methodological issues that remain relevant today. In short, the study examined compliance costs for a limited sample of communities and a select number of federal mandates and conditions of assistance. Of the hundreds of existing federal regulations that affect local expenditures, attention was focused on only six regulatory programs—each of which state and local officials had singled out as particularly expensive and intrusive.

The regulations selected for study were: advanced wastewater treatment requirements under the Clean Water Act Amendments of 1972 and 1977; unemployment compensation requirements for state and local employees under the 1976 Amendments to the Unemployment Insurance Compensation Act; bilingual education requirements (under various civil rights and bilingual education laws); P.L. 94-142, the Education of All Handicapped Children Act; transit accessibility requirements dictated by Section 504 of the 1973 Rehabilitation Act; and, minimum mandatory wage requirements under the Davis–Bacon Act. The seven jurisdictions included communities from all parts of the country, reflecting widely varying per-capita income levels and local tax burdens. Regulatory impacts were examined in six municipalities: Burlington, Vermont; Alexandria, Virginia; Cincinnati; Dallas; Seattle; and Newark, New Jersey. One urban county—Fairfax, Virginia—was also examined.

The research approach was relatively straightforward. Data were gathered from interviews with local officials and from local agency records. To compare expenses before and after the imposition of federal regulations, we supplemented government officials' subjective evaluation of "preferred costs" with trend data on expenditures. Because reliability was a greater concern than completeness in cost estimates, calculations were limited to the *incremental* costs of local compliance. The results typically did not factor in administrative or overhead costs; nor did they allow for the costs associated with secondary economic effects—all of which would have been extremely difficult to quantify. Thus, in a sense, the results understate the total regulatory costs associated with these six regulatory programs. However, because the benefits were not quantified, the results might also be seen as overstating costs.

To determine incremental costs, all direct local expenditures were identified under the six regulatory regimes that would not have been incurred in the absence of federal requirements. In other words, when existing local programs overlapped with federal requirements, only the proportion of total outlays that exceeded the level considered necessary by local officials were counted as costs. Thus, if local engineers believed secondary treatment of wastewater sufficient to meet health and safety objectives but federal standards required tertiary or advanced secondary treatment, only the differential between the two would be identified as an incremental cost.

FINDINGS

In brief, the regulations examined imposed substantial costs on the seven jurisdictions. The six mandates alone imposed an average cost of $25 per capita—an amount roughly comparable to the average federal revenue-sharing receipts of each site in 1978.

Jurisdictions varied substantially, with estimated costs ranging from $51.50 per capita in Newark, New Jersey to a low of $6 per capita in Burlington, Vermont. Four factors drove this variation in impact. First, and perhaps most important, is the *level of prior activity* conducted in each site in the specific area addressed by federal regulation. Cincinnati, for example, had a fully developed program for educating the handicapped in place at the time of enactment of the Education of All Handicapped Children Act. As a result, no incremental costs were incurred. Dallas, by contrast, had only a skeletal program, so costs soared after promulgation of federal standards.

Other factors contributing to variation include *local demographic characteristics*. Port and border cities such as Newark and Dallas have large non-English-speaking populations that require expensive bilingual programs. By contrast, cities farther inland tend to have more homogeneous populations and do not incur comparable costs.

Fiscal condition can also affect regulatory costs. For example, the burden of paying unemployment compensation tended to fall most heavily on cities like Newark, in the weakest fiscal conditions. Such cities are often hardest hit by economic downturns that compel widespread municipal layoffs. Ironically, then the cities and counties that are poorer and are suffering greater economic dislocation will have to bear heavier costs than more affluent jurisdictions. Hence, a key finding was that federal mandates appear to have regressive distributional effects—taxing poorer jurisdictions at a higher rate than richer ones.

These points, of course, represent only partial explanations for varying cost impacts. Others which would also influence outcomes include differences in climate and environmental conditions, in levels of political resistance to federal rules, and in levels of technical capability in understanding regulatory requirements and devising cost-effective compliance alternatives.

LIMITS OF THE STUDY

The study was limited in a number of ways—ways that suggest the difficulty of estimating mandate costs. In the first place, it examined only intergovernmental regulations that had been or were being implemented, making accurate assessments of incremental costs far easier than would be the case when speculating on prospective costs of proposed legislation or regulations. Second, it focused on a few discrete regulatory requirements in which total costs were typically absorbed—and could be identified—by a single governmental agency. The inquiry would have been much more difficult had it examined crosscutting requirements—which apply to all or many assistance programs. Along the same lines, even when measuring the rules that it did, the study was limited to direct compliance costs—it did not try to measure administrative or overhead expenses associated with compliance, much less the noneconomic costs. Finally, no attempt was made to identify or quantify benefits.

HIDDEN COSTS

Beyond these concerns, the report to the Joint Economic Committee pointed up problems that all efforts to calculate the costs associated with federal intergovernmental regulations would have to address.

First, costs of regulations mandating the provision of new services or goods (such as transportation for the handicapped) are frequently underestimated because that service or facility often induces new and unanticipated demand. To illustrate, in 1982, after Philadelphia's transit agency created a door-to-door paratransit service for the disabled in response to federal regulations, demand surged beyond all expected levels.[5]

Second, cost projections for regulations which compel major capital expenditures often underestimate associated operating and maintenance costs. A good example is the Safe Drinking Water Act regulations (see chapter 7).

Third, federal directives that stimulate a high level of demand for a product or service can produce significant price effects, often increasing total compliance costs, at least in the short run. This effect has been observed for a broad spectrum of goods and services, including sewage treatment equipment and health services.

FUTURE RESEARCH NEEDS

Clearly the state-level research reported elsewhere in this volume is valuable. However, we now need to deepen our understanding of mandates. What is needed are more cost-impact studies with a special focus on distributional issues. How have jurisdictions that are the least and the most able to pay fared in terms of costs arising from new regulations and from deregulation? And how do regulatory savings stack up against losses attributable to reductions in intergovernmental revenues?

Beyond these questions, we need an examination of policy changes at the state and local level in areas in which federal regulations have been eliminated or reduced. Are the rules of programs that have been substituted consistent with federal legislative objectives? Who are the winners and losers from intergovernmental deregulation? What have been the announced and actual achievements of these policies?

Notes

1. Thomas Muller and Michael Fix, "The Impact of Selected Federal Actions on Municipal Outlays," in U.S. Congress, Joint Economic Committee, Special Study on Economic Change, Vol. 5, *Government Regulation: Achieving Social and Economic Balance* (Washington, D.C.: U.S. Government Printing Office, 1980) p. 327.

2. 426 U.S. 833 (1976).

3. 469 U.S. 528 (1984).

4. Supra, note 1.

5. Michael Fix, Carol Everett, and Ronald Kirby, "Providing Public Transportation to the Disabled: Local Responses to Evolving Federal Policies" (Washington, D.C.: The Urban Institute, 1985), Project Report 3258-1.

Chapter Three

ESTIMATING THE IMPACT OF FEDERAL LEGISLATION ON STATE AND LOCAL GOVERNMENTS

Theresa A. Gullo

This chapter reviews the experience of CBO in preparing estimates of the costs that federal legislation imposes on state and local governments. The following discussion

□ provides an overview of the origin of CBO's involvement in preparing state and local cost estimates,

□ presents summary statistics on six years of state and local cost-estimating experience,

□ reviews CBO's estimating methodology and the major problems encountered, and,

□ speculates on the impacts of CBO's state and local estimates on congressional decisionmaking.

STATE AND LOCAL GOVERNMENT COST ESTIMATE ACT OF 1981: AN OVERVIEW

The State and Local Government Cost Estimate Act became law in December 1981.[1] It requires CBO to prepare estimates of the costs that would be incurred by state and local governments in complying with federal legislation that is reported from full committees in the House or Senate. The state and local cost estimates are to be included in committee reports along with the estimates of costs that would be incurred by the federal government, which CBO has been preparing since 1976. The new requirement took effect on October 1, 1982, and CBO prepared its first state and local cost estimate in November 1982.

The requirement that CBO prepare state and local cost estimates would have expired on September 30, 1987, but Congress indefinitely extended the requirement that same year.

The act requires CBO to prepare state and local cost estimates only for legislation likely to cost at least $200 million annually. Estimates are also required if legislation is likely to have exceptional fiscal consequences for a particular region or level of government. State and local estimates for appropriation or tax bills are not required.

Despite these limitations, CBO has adopted a policy of attempting to prepare state and local cost estimates for all authorizing bills that committees report. Because much of the work is done simply to determine whether the $200 million threshold is met, Congress is provided whatever information is gathered, regardless of the statutory threshold.

CBO integrates state and local estimates in its federal cost-estimate work: each cost analyst has primary responsibility for preparing both federal and state and local estimates for bills under his or her jurisdiction. No special state and local unit was created within CBO; instead people with backgrounds in state and local government finance were added to the staff. These specialists act as resource people for analysts in all policy/budget areas. They also prepare state and local cost estimates for legislation with major state and local impacts, such as the Fair Labor Standards Act and the Clean Air Act.

In terms of implementation, in preparing state and local estimates, CBO interprets costs as the direct budgetary costs or savings that would be incurred by state and local governments as a result of the legislation. This procedure is the equivalent of the direct budgetary costs and savings that CBO estimates for the federal government. CBO does not—in doing either federal or state and local cost estimates—try to estimate second-order effects of legislation, such as possible effects on state tax revenues as a result of a bill's impact on the economy.

SUMMARY OF CBO'S STATE- AND LOCAL-GOVERNMENT COST ESTIMATES

Over the past six years, CBO has prepared more than 3,500 state and local estimates, mostly for bills as they were reported from committee (see table 3.1). When requested, it provides federal and state and local estimates of bills at other stages of the legislative process: when bills are introduced, are reported from subcommittee, are being amended during floor consideration, and are in conference negotiations.

Table 3.1 STATE AND LOCAL COST ESTIMATES PREPARED: SIX YEARS OF
EXPERIENCE

Estimates Prepared	1983	1984	1985	1986	1987	1988	Total	Average
For bills reported from committee	483	554	367	465	393	559	2,821	470
Other formal estimates[a]	90	87	166	125	138	127	733	122
Total	573	641	533	590	531	686	3,554	592
Estimates with no impacts	496	584	488	543	448	598	3,157	526
(percentage of total)	87%	91%	92%	92%	84%	87%	89%	89%
Estimates with some impacts	77	57	45	47	83	73	382	64
(percentage of total)	13%	9%	8%	8%	16%	11%	11%	11%
Estimates with impacts above $200 million threshold	24	6	14	8	22	15	89	15
(percentage of total)	4%	1%	3%	1%	4%	2%	3%	3%

Source: Congressional Budget Office, Bill Estimates Tracking System.
a. When requested, CBO provides cost estimates for bills when they are introduced,
are reported from subcommittee, are amended during floor consideration, and when
they are in conference.

The vast majority of the 3,500 estimates concluded that there would
be no cost to state and local governments. Only about 380 involved
any costs or savings for state and local governments, and of these,
only 89 showed state and local costs in excess of $200 million per
year.

MAJOR CONCLUSIONS TO BE DRAWN
FROM OUR EXPERIENCES

Six years of experience in preparing state and local government cost
estimates led to the following conclusions about the process:

□ Cost impacts of bills are unique, and no single estimating meth-
odology is applicable to all bills.
□ Generalizations are difficult to make.
□ Information is scarce at the legislative stage of the process.
□ The task is large; the time is short.
□ Often CBO has no way of knowing whether the estimates have an
impact on congressional decisionmaking.
□ Despite the problems, state and local estimates are important and
valuable.

The remainder of this chapter provides some detail on these conclusions, using as examples some of the major state and local estimates prepared for the 99th and 100th Congresses.

METHODOLOGICAL PROBLEMS

Initially, CBO analysts hoped to develop certain databases or networks that would give them a head start on state and local estimates. This approach was not feasible, however, primarily because the range of issues and the diversity of the data required were simply too great to allow the creation of one comprehensive database or network of contacts that could be tapped routinely for all state and local estimates. For example, in the past few years, CBO has had to analyze the potential effects of immigration reform, safe drinking-water requirements, prohibitions against sex discrimination in pension plans, and requirements for handicapped access to voting facilities. And for each of these issues, it usually takes half a dozen or more calls to each state or locality to identify the appropriate contacts and data sources. The only instance in which staff people were able to develop a network of sorts was in 1987, when several important environmental quality bills were considered for reauthorization. Then a network of state and local environmental experts and administrators was established, and it was used time and again to provide information on local compliance costs.

Publications from interest groups like the National Conference of State Legislatures and the National League of Cities listing state and local officials and staff have been valuable starting points in identifying contacts. But, generally, each bill or subject area must be approached separately to identify and locate specific relevant information.

ESTIMATING DIFFICULTIES

In view of the diverse sources of data needed to estimate the aggregate costs to state and local governments and of the uncertainty surrounding most state and local officials' estimates—or, often, educated guesses—quantifying costs is frequently difficult. Even when the costs to an individual entity can be quantified, it is often difficult to generalize from these case-by-case data. As a result, the analysis is sometimes limited to identifying the general qualitative nature of a bill's impact and providing examples of costs to specific localities.

An example is estimating the state and local budget impacts of ensuring handicapped accessibility to voting places. State and local impacts of the bill varied widely, and it was not possible to gather sufficient data to estimate the aggregate cost nationwide. It quickly became clear that the costs for each state and locality would depend, among other things, on the definition of accessibility used by each jurisdiction, the extent of present accessibility, and the remedy selected.

Some states estimated that they would incur little or no costs, because they already mandated accessibility to polling places. Other jurisdictions used relatively few inaccessible polling locations, so their compliance costs were also not expected to be large. Some states and localities planned to meet the bill's standards by allowing the elderly or handicapped to transfer their registration to accessible facilities, thereby minimizing costs. On the other hand, some jurisdictions used the worst case scenario and estimated the costs of installing wheelchair ramps at all polling places.

Estimates for compliance with this bill ranged from $845 per county in Georgia (to transfer registration of handicapped voters to accessible facilities) to $10,000 in the city of Minneapolis alone (to install ramps in all polling places). Given this wide range of expected compliance costs and the few data points available, there was no way to estimate one aggregate cost figure validly. Instead, the estimate discussed the potential range of impacts and provided numerous examples.

DIFFICULTIES OF ESTIMATING IMPACTS AT THE LEGISLATIVE STAGE

Another problem stems from the fact that bill language is often vague or purposely broad, making it difficult to project future impacts at the time bills are considered. This point is particularly true when Congress gives executive agencies broad discretion to promulgate technical regulations at a later date, as it routinely does with agencies such as the Environmental Protection Agency (EPA). For many environmental mandates, Congress must necessarily give the agencies with the technical expertise a certain amount of flexibility in developing technical standards. The development of these standards takes a long time. When cost estimates are prepared, therefore, it is often difficult—if not impossible—for federal agencies to interpret the language and to predict what final regulations will look like before they begin the extensive regulatory development process. Consequently, it is virtually impossible for state and local governments to predict how they will comply or for CBO to estimate the cost implications.

The cost estimate prepared for the Federal Insecticide, Fungicide and Rodenticide Act Amendments is a good example of this uncertainty. Under the provisions of the bill, states would be required to take remedial action to reduce pesticide levels or prevent consumption of contaminated water when notified by EPA. The cost implications of this requirement were uncertain, depending upon how EPA would interpret the law in developing the regulations. If the requirements were interpreted broadly to require states to take specific steps to treat contaminated groundwater or to provide alternative drinking-water supplies, the costs could be extremely high. If, on the other hand, a more narrow interpretation were finally adopted, the total cost would not be as significant.

The point is that, in many instances, there is simply not enough information at the early stages of the process upon which to base a reliable quantitative estimate.

DIFFICULTIES ACCOMPLISHING THE TASK IN THE GIVEN TIME

Although in many ways CBO experiences are similar to those of state governments that prepare fiscal notes, the sheer magnitude of the task of estimating the impacts of federal mandates on the thousands of state and municipal governments is unique and staggering, making it difficult to provide timely estimates. Efforts to estimate the impacts of applying the Fair Labor Standards Act to state and local governments illustrate this problem.

In February 1985, the Supreme Court ruled in *Garcia v. San Antonio*[2] that the Fair Labor Standards Act (FLSA)[3] was applicable to state and local government employees. In the absence of congressional intervention, the *Garcia* decision could have made more than 7 million public employees in 50 states and approximately 3,000 counties, 19,000 municipalities, 17,000 townships, 15,000 school districts, and 29,000 local special districts legally entitled to overtime pay. Clearly, given the breadth of coverage, it was extremely difficult to estimate this impact quickly, completely, and precisely. Particularly because the impacts were expected to be largest at the municipal level, the sheer multitude of affected jurisdictions was staggering.

CBO has repeatedly found that the process does not lend itself well to the normal time frame for preparation of cost estimates of pending legislation. One of the objectives of the State and Local Government Cost Estimate Act was to include the state and local cost estimate in the committee report. Yet the committee report may be filed within hours after the committee has ordered the bill reported. Sometimes there is simply no time even to begin the state and local estimates. Then, analysts attempt to provide it later. But given the speed with which some bills are passed, amended, or voted down, it is not always possible to provide the state and local estimate in time for consideration on the House or Senate floor.

IMPACT OF CBO'S ESTIMATES: USEFUL INFORMATION, LIMITED INTEREST

What are the impacts of these state and local estimates? It is often difficult to know the impacts of a particular estimate. Members of Congress or committee staff seldom tell CBO the reasons for their decisions. In general, there is not a great interest in state and local estimates. If CBO does not provide a state and local estimate in time for the committee report, it is rarely asked to do so later. And there are rarely major controversies over the estimates.

Still, in a few instances, committee staff indicated that some estimates have affected congressional decisionmaking. For example, the House Committee on Education and Labor asked CBO in September 1985 to look into the FLSA issue as a way of helping it evaluate the need to introduce remedial legislation exempting state and local governments from complying. The committee staff remained interested in CBO staff progress and provided CBO with names of contacts and copies of estimates it had received from public interest groups, states, cities, and labor unions. CBO's preliminary estimate in mid-October put annual compliance costs at $0.5–$1.5 billion (the lower end of the range was provided to Congress by public interest groups, but it was twice as high as estimates from the labor unions). Although the efforts of public interest groups like the National League of Cities were certainly instrumental in the subsequent passage of remedial legislation, the committee staff told CBO that its estimate of costs became a baseline standard against which it weighed other information.

Another state and local estimate that seemed to have an impact dealt with education requirements for handicapped children between the ages of 3 and 5, as set forth in the Education of the Handicapped Amendments of 1986. Potential costs to states were estimated at $0.5–$2.7 billion. This estimate was based on discussions with 10–15 experts from state governments. The estimates CBO provided were controversial. However, based partly on the estimate, the bill was amended to reduce the potential costs to state government, and it was passed.

On the whole, the experience of providing state and local cost estimates has been a positive one for CBO and Congress. Clearly, Congress should—and, in reauthorizing the State and Local Cost Estimate Act has indicated its intent to—consider the potential cost ramifications for other governmental units when developing federal legislation. Despite the difficulty of the task, CBO cost estimates have generally provided unbiased and objective information necessary to allow Congress to assess these potential impacts on state and local governments.

CBO staff views state and local interest groups as a valuable resource and welcomes their input to the process.

Notes

1. P.L. 97-108.

2. Garcia v. San Antonio Metropolitan Transit Authority, 105 S. Ct. 1005 (1985).

3. 29 USC §§201 et seq.

Chapter Four

COST ESTIMATION AS AN ANTI-MANDATE STRATEGY

Ann Calvaresi Barr

BACKGROUND

At the request of Senator Dave Durenberger, GAO analyzed some of the techniques used by federal and state governments to address mandate burdens.[1] The primary objective was to determine what could be learned from state experiences that might be useful at the federal level.

The primary federal and state response to concerns about mandates has been to require the preparation of estimates of the cost impacts of proposed legislation on subordinate levels of government. At the federal level, the State and Local Cost Estimate Act of 1981 requires CBO to estimate costs for mandates contained in proposed federal legislation. The principal purpose of these estimates is to increase awareness among members of Congress of the costs state and local governments would incur if proposed legislation were adopted. Similar processes and purposes exist in 42 states.

OBJECTIVES, SCOPE, AND METHODOLOGY OF THE GAO REVIEW OF COST ESTIMATION APPROACHES AND IMPACTS

At the federal level, GAO reviewed CBO cost-estimation strategies and assessed their impacts on reducing mandates by talking with congressional staff and public interest groups. At the state level, GAO staff visited eight states to assess their cost-estimation strategies and sent questionnaires to state officials, legislative leaders and public interest groups representing local governments in all 50 states.

This chapter comments on three major areas:

☐ the experiences and reasonableness of the CBO approach to preparing state and local cost estimates,
☐ the impacts of federal and state cost-estimation processes on relieving the mandate burden imposed on subunits of government, and
☐ the features of state cost-estimation processes that might improve the usefulness of cost estimation as an antimandate strategy at the federal level.

CBO'S COST-ESTIMATION APPROACH: A COMPARISON WITH STATE PROCESSES

Based on the review and comparison with state processes, CBO does a reasonable job estimating the costs of mandates contained in proposed legislation, given the constraints under which it operates. These constraints are listed below.

The first constraint facing estimating units is limited time. On the federal level, CBO prepares estimates when bills are reported out of committee for inclusion in committee reports. Typically, CBO has less than five days to prepare an estimate. The majority of state cost-estimating units faced similar time constraints; over 50 percent of the state estimating units reported having five days or less to prepare their local cost estimates.

A second constraint emerges from the variety of subject matter that proposed legislation encompasses. On the federal level, a sample of eight CBO estimates from the 99th Congress reveals that bills subject to cost estimates covered a wide range of activities, including education, the environment, and labor standards, to name just a few. The review of state cost-estimation practices showed similar patterns.

A third constraint is the absence of meaningful databases that can be accessed for the preparation of state and local estimates. A state mandate study in Illinois recognized that cost estimation "is clearly a difficult task especially when there is no historical information on which to base the cost estimates . . . ."[2]

A fourth constraint worth noting is the competing priorities that cost-estimating units face. At CBO and the state level, respectively, estimating the federal and state costs of proposed legislation receives higher priority than estimating state and local costs of legislation. In the federal legislative process, bills will not be considered on the floor without a CBO estimate of the federal cost impact but can be considered without CBO state and local cost estimates. For example, during consideration of the Safe Drinking Water Act Amendments of 1986, the federal cost estimate was included in committee reports, but the state and local estimates were not available until after the bill passed.

As a result of the constraints listed above, estimating units must rely on a network of federal, state, and local officials knowledgeable about mandate areas who can provide relevant information quickly. This dependence represents the most reasonable and only practical approach to determining the likely state and local cost of new legislation containing mandates.

On the federal level, CBO does an impressive job identifying and contacting a mix of federal, state, and local officials that varies with each legislative proposal for which it prepares state and local cost estimates. CBO collects data through telephone contacts with several sources. As an example of the scope of CBO contacts made for the Safe Drinking Water Act Amendments, CBO analysts contacted (1) three committee staffs to obtain data sources, (2) Environmental Protection Agency and Office of Technology Assessment officials, because of their experience with safe drinking water standards, (3) two interest groups representing local water control agencies, and (4) twelve affected local public-water-treatment plants for cost data and overall comments on CBO's estimation approach.

Although the states also rely on telephone contacts with program officials, their range of contacts was typically not as impressive or as thorough as CBO's, despite the fact that CBO and the state estimating units face similar constraints. State agencies were the primary data sources used by state cost-estimating units.

COST ESTIMATION'S IMPACT ON MANDATES

A cost-estimation process produces valued sources of information, and the benefits of the processes outweigh the costs, as agreed by legislative committees at both the federal and state levels. However, it is only truly effective in deterring, modifying, or providing funding for mandates when there is strong legislative concern about the impacts of imposing mandates on lower levels of government.

Congressional staff values CBO's state and local estimates and agrees that CBO produces reliable and objective ones. The congressional staff also recognizes that, at the same time, state and local cost estimates usually do not influence changes in legislation either to reduce mandate burden or to provide mandate funding. More specifically, cost estimates had no effect on reducing mandates for five of eight legislative proposals reviewed at the federal level. There are three reasons.

First, committee staff said that programmatic and policy issues are usually of greater concern to federal legislators than are state and local costs. For example, the primary reason for the 1986 passage of the Safe Drinking Water Act Amendments imposing additional standards on local water systems was the need for clean drinking water. This factor overshadowed state and local cost considerations estimated by CBO to be $3.5 billion.

Second, federal policy debates focus primarily on federal, not state and local, costs. This focus often leads to mandates requiring state and local cost sharing. For example, two legislative proposals reviewed, the Housing Act of 1985 and the Water Resources Act of 1985, required state and local governments to share the costs of emergency shelters for the homeless and of water projects, respectively. Committee staffs said that cost sharing recognized the state and local character of these problems and the limited amount of federal funds.

Committee staff also said that CBO's state and local cost estimates are sometimes too late because they are prepared after bills are reported from committees, when most policy decisions have already been made. It must be noted here that this lag is not CBO's fault; CBO is required to prepare estimates at this time as directed in the authorizing statute—The Congressional Budget Act of 1974.

On the other hand, there were a few cases in which CBO's state and local estimates did influence Congress to reduce or fund mandates. There was strong congressional commitment, for example, to amend the Fair Labor Standards Act in order to lessen the state and local cost impact of the Supreme Court's *Garcia* decision, which applied federal overtime and minimum wage provisions to state and local governments. CBO was asked to do a special cost-impact analysis because legislators were being pressured by interest groups presenting conflicting cost-impact data.

Committee staff commented that CBO's $1.5 billion estimate promoted support for legislation that would reduce state and local costs by authorizing state and local governments to use compensatory time to reward employees working overtime rather than pay overtime. In effect, the cost estimate validated interest-group claims that the court's decision would have a significant cost impact on public employers.

Committee staff said that CBO's cost data were influential because (1) CBO had a credible and bipartisan reputation, particularly at a time when there were conflicting data; (2) the estimate was prepared prior to the committee's approval and report of the legislation, a point earlier than is required under the cost-estimate statute; and, (3) the pressure exerted by state and local interest groups during deliberations on the proposed amendment forced Congress to address state and local cost concerns.

SUGGESTIONS TO STRENGTHEN COST ESTIMATION'S IMPACT ON MANDATES

State cost-estimation processes generally produced impacts similar to those at the federal level, primarily increasing legislative awareness of local costs. There were, however, some attributes of state processes that, if used at the federal level, could focus more attention as well as promote greater legislative concern for federal legislation's impact on state and local government budgets. These attributes include preparing estimates earlier for important amendments to proposed bills and for all types of bills, including proposed tax and appropriation legislation.

The preparation of periodic reports estimating the total cost of mandates imposed by federal legislation on state and local governments would also be useful. Further, greater involvement by state and local interest groups during legislative deliberation could heighten legislators' awareness of the state and local cost impacts.

Prepare Estimates Earlier

When cost estimates are introduced into the legislative process can affect how legislators will use them. Seventy-three percent of the state cost-estimating units responding to the questionnaire said estimates were prepared before the full committee cleared bills—the time that normally triggers the preparation of CBO's estimates. Further questionnaire analysis shows that when cost estimates were prepared early in the legislative process, they were used to a greater extent than were those prepared later. Preparing state and local cost estimates earlier, that is before bills clear cognizant committees, will facilitate their use because they would be available before legislative decisions are made.

Prepare Estimates for Amendments

Preparing cost estimates for legislative amendments containing mandated state and local costs would help ensure that important changes were not overlooked. The questionnaire analysis shows that states reporting relatively high use of cost estimates were also states that usually prepared them for amendments. Similarly, states reporting some or no use of cost estimates were characteristically ones that seldom prepared cost estimates for amendments. CBO, unlike the states, does not routinely prepare estimates for amendments. Instead, it prepares them only when requested by committees having jurisdiction over a bill. Preparing estimates for amendments would provide updated information to legislators regarding state and local cost implications.

Prepare Estimates for All Types of Bills

At the federal level, tax and appropriation bills are excluded from coverage. The preparation of state and local cost estimates for provisions of tax and appropriation bills would provide cost-impact information on a broader range of mandates, thereby giving legislators a more complete picture of the potential mandate burden being imposed on state and local governments. State and local interest groups said that excluding such bills ignores substantial cost impacts passed on to state and local governments. For example, the National League of Cities said that the Tax Reform Act of 1986 contained federal reporting requirements that resulted in significant additional costs to local governments. On the state level, few estimating units exclude specific categories of bills from their process. For example, only 9 of the 44 state estimating units responding said that they, like CBO, exclude tax and/or appropriation bills from their processes.

Prepare Annual Reports

The preparation of a biennial report of federal legislation enacted during each Congress showing the total estimated cost impacts on state and local governments could help focus greater attention on total state and local cost burdens already mandated by federal legislation. At the federal level, a periodic report of this nature is not prepared. State and local interest groups said it is important to be aware of the total package of existing mandates when considering new legislation containing mandates. For instance, it would be useful to know that the most significant legislation containing mandates passed by the 99th Congress would cost state and local governments more than $2 billion annually, based on CBO's state and local estimates of committee-reported bills. Currently, CBO tracks all its estimates on a computerized system, which could serve as an initial database for preparing such a report.

Increase Public Interest Group Involvement

The involvement of interest groups in the legislative process can influence legislators' use of cost estimates. At the federal level, CBO's estimates had an impact on the course of the legislation associated with three bills when there was a high level of involvement by state and local governments and interest groups. In these cases, committee staff said that interest group involvement regarding cost issues caused legislators to focus greater attention on the cost estimates prepared for each bill and also influenced the final legislative outcomes. Other committee staff told us that state and local interest groups need to make themselves more visible on mandate issues. A recent research paper by James Kee and William Diehl also concluded that more should be done by these groups to track and influence potential mandate legislation.[3] At the state level, the degree of involvement by local interest groups also affected the legislators' use of cost estimates. Questionnaire results showed that cost estimates were used to a greater extent in states where local interest groups were reported by state officials to be more involved. Increased lobbying and organizational efforts with respect to proposed mandate legislation is needed to elevate legislative discussion on state and local cost concerns.

CONCLUSION

Cost estimates provide useful information to legislators, and the benefits of the processes appear to outweigh by far the costs associated with preparing them. Through adoption of the suggestions mentioned above, more attention would be focused on state and local cost issues at key points in the legislative process. Although it is not certain that these changes would lessen the overall mandate burden, it can be presumed that incorporating these features would enhance the commitment of legislators to addressing state and local concerns.

Notes

1. For a more detailed report of the study, see General Accounting Office, *Legislative Mandates: State Experiences Offer Insights for Federal Action* (Washington, D.C.: U.S. Government Printing Office, 1988), pp. 13–29.

2. Illinois Cities and Villages Municipal Problems Commission, *State Mandates Act: The First Year* (Springfield, Ill., 1981), p. 6.

3. James Edwin Kee and William Diehl, "Assessing the Costs of Federal Mandates on State and Local Government" (Washington, D.C.: Academy for State and Local Governments, 1988).

Chapter Five

STATE EXPERIENCES WITH MANDATE REIMBURSEMENT[1]

Richard H. Horte

BACKGROUND

In addition to study of the preparation of cost estimates (see chapter 4), GAO reviewed a second major step taken by several states, the establishment of mandate-reimbursement requirements. Essentially, such requirements provide that, when a government enacts mandates, it should pay for the costs it imposes on other levels of government.

Thirty-two states have formally considered mandate reimbursement; 14 have adopted a mandate-reimbursement requirement. In the other 18 states, the legislatures decided against it. The primary reasons were that states felt there simply was not enough money to cover a mandate-reimbursement program or that implementation costs would be too high. Some states are concerned about locking a state into such a requirement, particularly in a case when the state's fiscal condition is not favorable.

MANDATE BURDEN REDUCED BUT RESULTS VARY AMONG STATES

For the 14 states that adopted reimbursement, this strategy had greater impact on unfunded mandates than did the practice of estimating costs. It should be noted, however, that the impact overall was still considered relatively low. Reimbursement was simply not viewed as the solution to the problem. Further, the results have been rather mixed among the states.

Three outcomes were expected as a result of reimbursement. Obviously, one would be to fund the mandates. Two other expected outcomes were that mandates would be deterred—states would stop passing mandates—or they would modify the mandates in some way that would significantly lessen the burdens on local government.

Funding has not been a significant result of mandate reimbursement. It was significant only in California, which, by 1987, had paid out about $2 billion through its mandate-reimbursement program. But that fact must be viewed in context: California has operated a reimbursement program for about 15 years, beginning in 1973, when many mandates were being enacted at both the federal and state levels. As a result, California found itself paying for a lot of mandates. The state was also in a healthy fiscal climate and was not too concerned about paying for mandates. That attitude has had a cumulative effect over the years. It is still paying for many of those mandates adopted years ago.

California is mentioned here simply because when one thinks of mandate reimbursement, that's the first state they consider. Some of the perceptions that people have about mandate reimbursement are based on their understanding of California, namely, that reimbursement is going to cost a lot.

In contrast, the next largest mandate-reimbursement state was Massachusetts. In 1987, California paid about $144 million on about 60 mandates. Massachusetts paid about $5 million on 6 mandates.

The key point is that reimbursement helps deter mandates. The study looked at 7 of the 14 states with reimbursement requirements; of the 7, 4 (California, Massachusetts, Michigan, and Tennessee) were classified as having experienced some impact as a result of mandate reimbursement. The impact is primarily deterrence, stopping the legislature from passing or perhaps even introducing mandates. In the other three states (Colorado, Florida, and Illinois), the requirements had little impact on the passage or funding of mandates. Despite the existence of the requirement, mandates were still being passed and were not being funded.

Why does this situation occur? Why do the states vary so?

LEGISLATIVE PRIORITIES, OTHER FACTORS AFFECT OUTCOME

The major lesson learned from these states is that when a process resulted in reducing unfunded mandates, it was coupled with strong legislative concern. Essentially, it was the same situation as that of cost estimating. At the same time, certain factors seemed to prompt legislative support. In the four states where the requirements had greater impact, they had generally been initiated through constitutional amendment. In Massachusetts, the requirement was statutory but was based on an initiative instituted by the voters. In the other three states, where the requirement had little impact, the provision was statutory and originated within the legislature itself. Then the legislature can formally override the requirement at any time or it can simply ignore the requirement.

A state's willingness to fund mandates can also be affected by its fiscal condition. Massachusetts experienced a healthy fiscal climate following the introduction of its reimbursement program. Although California has paid significant amounts, its response to funding has risen and declined in relation to the state's fiscal condition.

Some states have given local governments the right not to comply with state mandates unless the state provides funding for the mandates. This feature is commonly referred to as optional compliance, which can place added pressure on the legislature to fund the cost of mandates if it wishes to ensure that all local governments comply. This right of optional compliance, in effect, can give the local governments new leverage in dealing with the state legislature to ensure that they do get funding. If they do not, they are under no obligation to carry out the mandate.

Despite these positive outcomes that have occurred at least to some extent in several states, certain negative effects seem to cut across almost all the states visited. The fact that the strategy is termed mandate reimbursement would seem to suggest that, if a mandate passes, it will be funded. Quite simply, that has not been the case even in states where mandate-reimbursement legislation is considered to have some positive impact.

Several factors account for this situation. The most important ones are highlighted below.

First, the definition of a mandate. Definitions vary from one state to another. Some states have a narrow definition of what constitutes a mandate. For example, Michigan does not provide reimbursement for any mandate that affects both the public and private sectors. That provision may not apply in other states. What may be a reimbursable mandate in one state may not be in another state; yet it is still a mandate.

Second, exemption authority. Several states include in their requirements the right of the legislature to exempt the state from providing funding under certain circumstances. Perhaps such authority may be necessary, but it can be abused.

By 1987, Illinois had passed about 60 mandates since it adopted a mandate-reimbursement requirement. Of those 60, the state has actually exempted itself from being subject to reimbursement for about half. The other half, however, have not been paid for. Why aren't local governments doing anything about this situation, like taking the state to court? In one case, they tried. They went to court and won. The state court ruled that if they were not being paid, they did not have to carry out the mandate; it is an option. The state response was then to exempt the mandate from reimbursement so that local governments would have to carry out the mandate. They have not since gone to court.

Third, the funding mechanism itself. In some cases, funds are provided simply by earmarking some portion of what is considered local aid or general revenue sharing. If a state merely earmarks funds that are coming from another source as opposed to providing new funds, then the state is really not accomplishing the objective of mandate reimbursement.

Fourth, the timing of funding. In Massachusetts, for example, appropriations are up front. That is the only way a feature such as optional compliance can work. In California, however, funding is provided on a reimbursement basis; funding can occur long after the mandate is implemented. Local governments carry out mandates, submit claims, and hope to get paid. In the meantime, they must carry out the mandate; they have no option.

One final issue at the state level is the impact of the courts. To the extent that issues are not resolved when the mandate-reimbursement requirement is established, they will be left for court interpretation. Decisions go either way, supporting local government in some cases and the state in others. The concern here is simply that, if there is a mandate-reimbursement requirement, then the state and local governments should try to resolve issues, especially the definitional issues, up front as much as possible to avoid having the courts take over administration of the program.

OUTLOOK FOR REIMBURSEMENT AT THE FEDERAL LEVEL

That discussion brings us to the federal level. The study objective was to look at these state programs to see what could be learned about their application at the federal level. Although reimbursement programs have somewhat reduced the number of unfunded state mandates, it seems unlikely, at least at the present time, that a similar reimbursement requirement would be workable at the federal level, given the continued existence of large federal budget deficits, the absence of strong voter pressure to reduce the impact of mandates, and the perception that certain actions need to be mandated by the federal government to ensure uniform application by the states.

At the federal level, fiscal condition is certainly a key factor. At the state level, fiscal condition was important in making this program work. At the federal level, during times of large budget deficits, Congress is less likely to authorize reimbursement for expenses incurred by state and local governments to comply with federally mandated actions.

In this environment, the pressure can increase to enact mandates prescribing national policy without funding. Some states have sought to protect local governments from unfunded mandates by making local compliance optional, rather than by providing funding. Faced with continued budget deficits, federal officials could provide the same option to state government. Although this action might be advantageous to states, it could also be viewed as an unacceptable option at the federal level, because it could well result in the mandate being ignored. The federal government has sought to ensure in many areas at least a minimum level of benefit or protection for people in all states. Optional compliance with federal mandates could erode the capability of the federal government to accomplish these and other similarly important purposes.

Where do we go from here? First, consider some of the points raised in chapter 4 on cost estimates. Perhaps the first step needs to be more consciousness raising on the part of state and local interest groups working with congressional committees to promote consideration of state and local costs.

Second, at the state level, studies have attempted to summarize total costs. Some states have set up commissions that have looked into this issue and have tried to bring to the forefront what mandates are costing.

These are two of the first steps that ought to be tried before the federal government gets locked into a reimbursement requirement, particularly at a time of federal budget deficits, when many attempts may be made to avoid carrying out such a statutory requirement.

Note

1. For a more detailed report of the study, see General Accounting Office, *Legislative Mandates: State Experiences Offer Insights for Federal Action* (Washington, D.C.: U.S. Government Printing Office, 1988), pp. 30–44.

Chapter Six

ASSESSING THE EXTENT OF THE MANDATE PROBLEM IN SOUTH CAROLINA

Janet M. Kelly

The South Carolina Advisory Commission on Intergovernmental Relations (SCACIR) periodically asks local government leaders to describe the more difficult aspects of their jobs. The inquiries, always informal, begin with a general discussion of the inherent problems with local policy made at the state house rather than the courthouse. They progress to a serious discussion of the worst problem facing cities and counties in South Carolina. The scenery changes, but the script stays the same.

"It's the mandates that are killing us," they say. "Which ones?" we ask. "All of them." Too many times SCACIR dodged the issue by saying it cannot be expected to respond to a problem that it can't define. But that is just what they expected SCACIR to do. Eighteen months after the commission had generously granted staff its full support of a comprehensive mandates project, the recommendations were published.[1] For the first time, it was clear that the answer so often given was right on target. The real problem with state mandates to local government *is* "all of them."

The mandates study began with deliberation over the best working definition of a mandate. The U.S. Advisory Commission on Intergovernmental Relations (ACIR) focused on the substitution of state priorities for local priorities as a basis for examining the scope and influence of mandates. It defined a mandate as a "legal requirement, constitutional provision, statutory provision, or administrative regulation—that a local government undertake a specific activity or provide a service meeting minimum state standards."[2]

Equally important and frequently ignored are the mandates that *prevent* the local government from undertaking an activity or providing a service. Called restrictive mandates, these laws and regulations limit the locality's ability to make decisions about which programs and services it will provide and, most especially, how it will pay for them. The combined impacts of an active mandate as defined by the ACIR and a restrictive mandate as defined by SCACIR can be devastating. The state can require a new activity or service standard, provide no reciprocal funds, and prevent the local government from raising taxes to pay for the new mandate.

Alert for both active and restrictive mandates, an industrious law student pored over the South Carolina Code of Laws and Agency Regulations for six weeks. A total of 608 legislative mandates have been enacted. Only 34 had been repealed or found unconstitutional, leaving South Carolina localities with 574 legislative mandates with which to comply. The first, appearing in the late seventeenth century, prohibits worldly work on Sunday except by those who practice a faith that observes Saturday as the Sabbath and who happen to reside in Charleston County. One of the latest involves the distribution of assets seized during arrests for trafficking in illegal substances. There were 72 state agency mandates to local governments, all of them enforceable. Most come from the Department of Health and Environmental Control and regulate health care, disease control, inspection of public areas and products, and water and waste disposal systems.

Some decades have seen a greater proliferation of mandates than others. The first dramatic increase in legislatively enacted mandates occurred in 1961–70. Seventy-one mandates were enacted then—about seven per year. The following decade, 1971–80, 105 mandates were enacted, approximately 10 per year. In 1983, the legislature passed a fiscal note bill. It required that the financial impact of any mandate to local government be assessed before the legislature acts upon the bill. Since 1983, the average number of mandates enacted per year rose from 10 to about 14. Why the increase when the fiscal note bill was designed to inhibit passage of mandates? The answer is simple. The bill was not complied with, at least not in spirit. Of the 19 mandates with identifiable local costs that came before the legislature between 1984 and 1986, only 6 had fiscal notes attached. These 6 addressed the cost of the mandates to the state, not to the local government.

But the failing of the fiscal note bill is certainly not the reason for the many mandates facing localities. Mandates become a part of the local burden in other ways than directly through the legislature. There are pass-through mandates from the federal government, usually for environmental protection and sanitary standards (although South Carolina usually enhances these mandates and passes them along as state mandates). There are mandates by budget proviso—riders, if you will—to the state budget bill that make funding for localities and agencies serving localities contingent upon local compliance with some standard. These mandates are temporary unless they reappear in the next year's appropriations act.

Finally, there are mandates that are not mandates at all. Traditional mandates exist in custom rather than in law. South Carolina counties named these traditional mandates as the more burdensome of the lot. When a circuit court judge demands a new gavel and a vending machine, the county complies with a soft grumble. When the local division of the state welfare office needs new computers and telephones, or worse, more office space, the county demands some limit to its responsibility.

Although budget proviso mandates and traditional mandates are important contributors to the whole mandates problem in South Carolina, their transient nature does not allow them to be catalogued and organized by function the way legislative and agency mandates can. They were described anecdotally and through attitude survey results. Legislative and agency mandates were carefully organized by the purpose they served and were combined to generate an important research tool—the catalog of existing state mandates to local governments.

From the catalog, it is apparent that most state mandates apply to counties (93%) and have to do with the day-to-day operations of government (35%). These general government mandates are not a part of a greater social welfare agenda. They are rules that govern the transaction of local government business. The next largest group of mandates involves public safety and transportation, followed by mandates on public education. Even though safety and education mandates suggest social goal setting, most of the mandates are rather about record keeping, fee and fine amounts, and other administrative matters.

The cost-analysis portion of the study, contracted out to the Bureau of Governmental Research and Service of the University of South Carolina, took a stratified sample of cities and counties and assessed the marginal and total costs of selected mandates.[3] It made three important contributions to the study. First, it offered evidence of a long standing local complaint—that state-shared revenue is not sufficient to cover the cost of state-imposed mandates. Second, the financial burden of mandates falls most heavily on those localities least able to bear it. Finally, the biggest problem is the number of mandates and the "cumulative effect of years of incremental change." Loosely translated, that means that the problem is "all of them."

The issue, it seems, is one of perspective. South Carolina frames the problem in micro terms (effects of an individual mandate) and localities see the macro picture (the cumulative effect of all mandates). The state and the localities have no substantive disagreement over the micro issues. Any given mandate will have served a purpose or currently serves a purpose of making local government better. Is any mandate totally outrageous? No. Are mandates expensive? Sometimes. Does that expense cripple the local budget? No. Would some localities, in the absence of certain mandates, fail to meet the standard that the mandates require? Probably. Is it necessary to look at ways to relieve the mandate burden in South Carolina? From the micro perspective, it is not. But from the macro or local perspective, the cumulative and insidious impact of 646 state mandates makes a new mandates policy for the future imperative.

Local officials in South Carolina believe that the state has a legitimate role in the operation of local government. But they also believe that because so many of South Carolina's mandates are procedural—designed to enhance local accountability—the intended effect and the actual effect often differ. The disparity arises when the cumulative impacts of mandates are ignored.

What has been accomplished by this study? For the first time, approximately how many mandates there are, what they were intended to accomplish, and whom they affect are known. The fiscal impact law has not inhibited the passage of legislative mandates. The study debunked the myths that the localities face a manageable number of state mandates and receive adequate funding for them. Localities resent the inefficiencies that result from so many mandates, not the goal that the mandates were intended to achieve. It was demonstrated that a local burden exists when mandates compete and conflict. Finally, the study recommended practical steps to relieve that burden and keep it manageable in the future.[4]

Maybe most important, the study created the possibility of an informed dialogue between the state and its localities. Maybe it fostered a better spirit of cooperation as legislators understand local issues and local leaders understand the state's desire for conformity and accountability. Additionally, SCACIR learned to be a better listener. South Carolina's cities and counties intuitively understood something that it took the staff 18 months to demonstrate. The real problem with state mandates is "all of them."

Specific policy recommendations from the SCACIR study are:

□ Future mandates should be incorporated into the existing catalog at the end of each two-year legislative session and their fiscal notes retained for the record.

□ As new approaches and techniques for assessing the costs of mandates are developed, they should be used to study local government costs.

☐ Existing mandates should be subject to a periodic review of their relevance. Mandates that are archaic, not implemented, not enforced, or unclear should be either removed from the code or revised and enforced.

☐ Fiscal note legislation should be complied with in the spirit in which it was enacted. The notes should reflect the costs to local governments as well as to the state and should accompany each legislative and agency mandate.

☐ The fiscal note should be prepared by a neutral, quantitatively sophisticated group. That group should conduct periodic internal validity studies that compare their estimated economic impacts of mandates with the actual economic impacts. Predictions should include the cumulative impacts of the proposed mandate. When a previous mandate competes with or limits ability to comply with a proposed mandate, a resolution should be offered.

☐ Existing fiscal note legislation should be amended to require a statement by its author as to how the mandate is to be funded.

☐ Local government officials should be permitted to appeal a prospective mandate and present an independent assessment of its cumulative economic impacts to the appropriate legislative committee before a mandate is enacted.

☐ State government should clarify local government responsibilities regarding traditional mandates such as provision of office space and supplies to state agencies.

☐ Mandates should exist in one of three forms: legislative enactment, administrative regulation, and executive order. Although there may be good reason to include a mandate to local government in the budget bill one year, mandates by budget proviso should not recur.

☐ The state should consider the impact of federal pass-through mandates on localities, especially those that relate to water, air, and landfill standards, and should work with local officials to find creative ways to fund compliance.

Notes

1. Janet M. Kelly, *State Mandated Local Government Expenditures and Revenue Limitations in South Carolina* (Columbia: South Carolina Advisory Commission on Intergovernmental Relations, 1988).

2. Advisory Commission on Intergovernmental Relations, *State Mandating of Local Expenditures* (Washington, D.C.: U.S. Government Printing Office, 1978), p. 2.

3. Jane Massey and Edwin Thomas, *State Mandated Local Government Expenditures and Revenue Limitations in South Carolina: Part Four—Cost Analysis* (Columbia: Bureau of Governmental Research and Service, University of South Carolina, 1988).

4. For further reading, see Janet M. Kelly "State Mandated Local Government Expenditures and Revenue Limitations in South Carolina" in *Mandates: Perspectives from the States*, Jane Roberts, ed., (Washington, D.C.: Advisory Commission on Intergovernmental Relations, forthcoming).

Chapter Seven

THE SAFE DRINKING WATER ACT: A CASE STUDY

Arnold M. Kuzmack

This chapter presents the implementation of the Safe Drinking Water Act Amendments of 1986[1] as a case study of a federal mandate affecting state and local governments. In most case studies, you find out at the end how it comes out. But we don't know yet about this one.

This chapter is the first half of the case study, so to speak. It is interesting that only a couple of months ago the author became aware of the mandates problem. To some degree, to focus on a problem, one has to name it. We have had homeless people for hundreds of years, but suddenly in the last few years we have the "homeless problem." And, perhaps we are in a similar situation with the mandates problem.

In the drinking water program, the Environmental Protection Agency (EPA) has been off in its own little corner trying to cope with what Congress told it to do, dealing a lot with its state and local counterparts and their organizations. But state and local officials are in their own little corner as well. For example, state program officials do not have much sense of what the overall state fiscal situation is except as it affects their immediate budgets. In this respect, EPA officials are not much different from those who are charged with implementation of other federal programs.

This chapter first sets the stage by describing the program and then presents EPA cost estimates and their derivation. It then discusses the problems with implementing the mandate and the kinds of strategies with which EPA is struggling.

The basic institutional roles for the program are established by the statute. The job of the federal government is to set the drinking water quality standards. Implementation of those standards is then delegated to the states, in what has been called the partial preemption strategy. If a state is unwilling or unable to undertake this role, EPA implements the program in that state and directly regulates its public water supplies.

The Safe Drinking Water Act, originally enacted in 1974,[2] was the first statute in the environmental area in which it was envisaged that the states would have a lot of management flexibility in how they implemented the program. This approach has been picked up since then in other environmental legislation. The earlier statutes had many provisions stipulating that EPA had to approve everything the state did or that EPA could disapprove individual actions related to individual polluters, etc.

EPA is pleased that it has delegated the program to 54 of the 57 states and territories, and one more is working on it. That is a good record of establishing a relationship of sufficient trust that states are willing to accept responsibility for the program.

The public water systems' responsibilities are (1) to comply with the chemical and biological standards that are set and (2) to pay for the necessary improvements. The Safe Drinking Water Act does not provide for a federal subsidy of any sort to the public water systems. Some other federal programs, each with its own statutory objectives and restrictions, could incidentally contribute, such as the Department of Housing and Urban Development, the Economic Development Administration, and the Farmers Home Administration, but no program is specifically directed toward offsetting the costs of compliance with the requirements of the Safe Drinking Water Act. Moreover, the funding levels for these other programs have been significantly reduced in recent years. (EPA does provide federal grant funds to offset partially state costs of implementing the administrative requirements of the program, taking enforcement actions, etc.)

The entities regulated by the program are public water systems. The law defines a public water system as an entity providing piped water for human consumption to 25 or more people or to 15 or more service connections.

EPA has defined several categories of public water systems: approximately 60,000 community water systems serve residential populations; another 20,000 or so that EPA calls nontransient systems serve the same people day after day for long periods, such as schools and factories that have their own water systems; and more than 100,000 noncommunity water systems that include restaurants, highway rest stops, and the like, which have their own water supplies and serve 25 or more people per day. Technical requirements vary among these types of systems because the nature and duration of exposure to contaminants are different. This chapter concentrates on community water supplies.

The distribution by population served of the nation's community water supplies is an essential aspect of the program's implementation. About 6 percent of the systems serve 10,000 or more people each, and together they serve 78 percent of the people served by public water systems.

On the other side of the distribution, two-thirds of the systems serve fewer than 500 people each, and together they serve 2.5 percent of the population. One-third serve fewer than 100 people. These are obviously very different entities from the large systems.

The large systems are usually municipally owned, though some are investor owned and their rates are regulated by public utility commissions. (The same water quality standards apply to both publicly and privately owned systems, because of their common goal to protect public health.)

The large systems typically use surface water as their source, although some use groundwater. They all have professional management staffs with the expertise to operate water systems and an understanding of the technical requirements imposed upon them.

In contrast, the systems serving fewer than 100 or fewer than 500 people do not have such staffs and may have no operator at all. Most are either trailer parks that have their own wells serving a number of trailers or small subdivisions in which the developer built a common well instead of putting in individual wells. There is a resident manager or a homeowners' association that calls a plumber when the pump breaks down.

Obviously, these organizations differ from the large systems, with no technical capacity to understand or implement regulations and with little economic base to pay for needed improvements. They are typically not owned by a municipality, and they almost always use groundwater as their source (fortunately, because it is usually better than surface water). They usually provide either no treatment of the water at all or just disinfection, which is the bare minimum of treatment.

The costs that these systems charge vary considerably. Over half the systems charge less than $200 per family annually. But a significant number of systems, about 7 percent, are charging more than $500 per family per year with some as high as $1,000 per family per year. This range is used here as a benchmark—about the limit of what you can reasonably expect people to pay for water.

Following this brief description of the public water systems subject to EPA regulations is a description of the statutory mandate that EPA received from Congress in the Safe Drinking Water Act Amendments of 1986.

In brief, the law requires EPA to set a lot more drinking water standards. In part, this mandate reflects the wave of public concern and outrage over contamination resulting from hazardous waste disposal. In part, it reflects congressional dissatisfaction with the slow pace of standard setting prior to the amendments.[3] And, in part, it also reflects the distrust of EPA following the Ann Burford era, so that mandates given the agency allowed little flexibility. For example, EPA was given a list of 83 contaminants to regulate within three years. It is required to regulate 25 additional contaminants every three years, indefinitely. Thus, there will be many more drinking water standards for the states to implement and the public water systems to comply with.

EPA has estimated, as well as it can, the costs of compliance with all these regulations. What follows is, first, a description of the total national costs imposed on the public water systems, many of which are owned by local governments. In fact, the regulations impact differently on the large and the small systems.

The basic methodology is fairly simple in concept: estimate the number of systems (by size category) that would exceed the proposed standard, estimate what it would cost them to comply, and multiply these numbers. Performing the calculations obviously requires a lot of information as input. The quality of that information varies considerably, from data based on formal random surveys to best professional judgment as to the choices that will be made by the systems.

As always, some significant uncertainties in these analyses result from uncertainties in the input data. In addition, there is an inherent upward bias in regulatory cost estimates in general because the methodology always costs out an assumed set of actions that would comply with the regulation, but the regulated communities can often come up with other cheaper ways of achieving compliance.

Table 7.1 presents EPA's latest estimates of the total costs of compliance by the public water systems for regulations that are currently under development. It is revised from time to time.

The total capital cost adds up to $6 to 7 billion. Operating costs are also quite significant for some of the regulations. Thus, EPA will be adding close to $2 billion per year to the costs faced by public water systems, which will, of course, be paid by consumers. In addition, an estimate for the disinfection byproducts regulation is not

Table 7.1 TOTAL COSTS OF COMPLIANCE FOR COMMUNITY WATER
SYSTEMS, APRIL 1989

Regulation	Total capital costs	Total annualized costs
Volatile organics	$ 164	$ 56
Filtration	2,642	586
Lead	933	335
Radionuclides	1,142	210
Other chemicals	400	106
Disinfection	1,352	488
Total	$6,633	$1,781

Source: EPA estimates

shown; it is several years away and cannot be estimated at this time, although the costs could be substantial. Assuming that it would cost a significant fraction of $1 billion per year, the total compliance cost would be in the range of $2 to 3 billion per year.

It is important to point out that these impacts will fall unevenly on the public water systems. If a system measures the level of a contaminant and finds that it does not exceed the standard, then it will not be necessary to pay for treatment to remove it. Moreover, the large systems will face different kinds of contamination problems from the small systems.

The large systems will be impacted most by three of the regulations: filtration, lead, and disinfection byproducts. Some will be in compliance with all three with little additional cost. Others could face capital costs in the hundreds of millions of dollars. Even in the worst case, however, the annual increases in family water bills appear to be relatively small, say, $50 per family per year, a level that is clearly affordable.

The small and very small systems will face a different range of problems. Many will have to add disinfection and treatment to reduce lead levels, and large numbers will have to treat to remove radon. The cost of removing all three of these substances, in the smallest systems, is about $300 per family per year, a level that is considerable but may still be considered affordable. Beyond these, the rest of the 100-plus contaminants EPA will be regulating will occur at levels over the standards in only a few percentage or less of the systems. There are sure to be some systems that are unlucky enough to have to add two or three types of treatment at a cost that could reach well beyond any reasonable definition of affordability.

Thanks to economies of scale, these high costs occur only in systems serving fewer than 1,000 people. The act provides reasonable relief for these systems through variances and exemptions while giving their customers the best water quality they can afford.

While the amendments were being considered in Congress, EPA was well aware of the potential economic impacts on the systems. It worked with CBO, which developed a worst-case estimate of $3 billion per year. This is somewhat higher than EPA's current estimate, several years later.

Something that neither EPA nor anyone else focused on at the time is the state administrative costs of implementing all of these regulations. To some degree, this is how things were done pre-Gramm–Rudman: the presumption was that, if Congress imposed a new mandate, a reasonable amount of additional federal resources, including grants to states, would be forthcoming. It usually did work out that way.

EPA now has some estimates of these costs. The states are currently spending about $95 million on the program, of which the agency is providing about one-third through state program grants. It is estimated that total state spending would have to more than double to implement the new regulations fully. Post-Gramm–Rudman, increases in federal grants will not cover more than a fraction of the shortfall, even in the most optimistic case. (After passage of the amendments, there was one increase of $5 million in the grants in the FY 1987 appropriation. A proposed additional $5 million increase in FY 1988 was finally rejected in conference, and no increase was provided in FY 1989. An increase of $7 million was included in the president's FY 1990 budget.)

Regulations do not implement themselves. Without an adequate response to the shortfall in state resources for this program, the improvements in drinking water quality that Congress wanted will not be achieved, particularly in the small systems that will not know what to do unless they get a lot of assistance from the states. This situation is perhaps the most serious problem facing the program at this time. Although EPA does not have a complete answer, it and its state counterparts are grappling with the problem. Below is a brief indication of some of the directions EPA is pursuing.

EPA is trying to formulate its regulations in such a way as to minimize the state's transaction costs without compromising the health protection provided. The goal is to make the procedural aspects of the regulations as unburdensome as possible.

EPA is doing a lot to reach interest groups in addition to the ones it normally deals with, such as those representing the water suppliers and the state administrators of drinking water programs. For example, EPA discovered an association for mobile home parks. It needs to get them into the game, so to speak, to inform them about the requirements of the program and to solicit their help in informing their constituencies so that these systems can be motivated to comply voluntarily.

For the states to be able to cope with this workload, EPA is encouraging them to develop their own approaches, some of which the agency would not have been able to foresee. It hopes to be able to suggest some, to develop ways of exchanging experiences among the states, and generally to tap into the creativity that they have.

There have already been a number of innovative state approaches. New Jersey has actually imposed a tax on water provided by public water systems to fund its oversight programs. Minnesota came close to passing such a tax but, instead, increased program funding from general revenues. Many more of the states will probably be able to make use of user fees to offset their costs partially or stop providing certain services that they have been providing free, particularly for those larger systems that can pay for them.

As a last resort, EPA will be fairly explicit with the states as to which health threats are the highest priorities that should be controlled at the expense of not dealing with the others, if need be. Obviously, in that case, not all the regulations will be complied with—an unwelcome situation. But society would at least get the greatest public health pay off for the resources that it has been willing to devote to the enterprise of providing safe drinking water.

This description relates to the general issue of federal mandates. It is clear that the 1986 Amendments to the Safe Drinking Water Act will impose large increases in the costs faced by the states (the vast majority of them) that have chosen to accept primary enforcement authority for the program. It is unlikely that increases in the federal program grants will offset more than a fraction of these costs. Moreover, many public water systems, whether owned by local governments or private organizations, will face increased costs for water treatment that will be paid for by their customers, generally with no federal subsidy.

Thus, there appears to be a classic case of an unfunded federal mandate imposed on state and local governments. There is, however, another way of looking at this and other mandates. The members of Congress who passed the law were elected by the same voters who elect state legislators and other officials. They believed, presumably, that it is in the interest of their constituents to improve the level of protection of drinking water supplies. The costs of this or any other federal mandate will, one way or another, be paid by the people. For each such program, there may be strong arguments for or against paying the costs from the federal budget. It is hard to see, however, why this should always or even usually be the preferred policy.

Notes

This chapter was written by Dr. Kuzmack in his private capacity. No official support or endorsement by the Environmental Protection Agency or other agency of the federal government is intended or should be inferred.

1. P.L. 99–339.

2. P.L. 93–523.

3. See, for example, statement by Senator Dave Durenberger, *Congressional Record*, pp. S6397–98, 16 May 1985.

Chapter Eight

THE MASSACHUSETTS MANDATE STATUTE AND ITS APPLICATION

Emily D. Lunceford

This chapter explains how the Massachusetts mandate statute came about and how it functions; gives a nutshell summary of the law, what it requires, major elements of mandate findings, and exceptions to the general mandate-funding rule; and briefly describes other functions of the Division of Local Mandates (DLM).

The Massachusetts mandate statute came about as part of what is called the Citizens Taxpayer Revolt, Proposition 2½, similar to the Proposition 13 initiative in California.[1] It was overwhelmingly approved at the general election in November 1980. Particularly interesting, and very important to the administration of the mandate statute, is that the voters adopted this initiative after the legislature had had the opportunity first to act on bills that would have accomplished similar aims. The house and the senate both rejected proposals to implement a version of Proposition 2½, which also included a section to create a DLM and the mandate-funding rules that now govern legislation and regulations in Massachusetts.

The local mandate statute is an important element of what some call the Proposition 2½ success story in Massachusetts. Opponents of the tax reform measure argued before the fact that it would bankrupt local governments. Vastly increased amounts of local aid, general revenue sharing from the state government to cities and towns, were probably the major reason for the success story. The fact that Massachusetts has a local mandate statute requiring state funding of new programs is almost an equally important element of the fact that cities and towns have not gone bankrupt—and still continue to provide a reasonable level of public services at the local level in Massachusetts. Recent limits on the growth in state tax revenues[2] and a number of major new state programs, however, are likely to inhibit the legislature's ability to continue the trend of large annual local aid increases. Predictably, this may result in more municipal court challenges to unfunded state mandates.

The Bay State local mandate law is prospective. It constrains state activities imposing costs on local governments that take effect on or after January 1, 1981. The original version of the citizens initiative would have had the Commonwealth paying for all mandates, even those enacted prior to 1981. That requirement was easily seen as unworkable. Accordingly, the first year after the statute was enacted, the legislature made several corrective amendments. One was to insert the January 1, 1981, trigger date. This was reasonable, because the problem of identifying past mandates and the cost of assuming them were prohibitive. Further, by having a certain trigger date of January 1, 1981, the legislature and state agencies were now on notice that the rules were different, and they would have to think carefully about the local impact before they would act.

In summary, this mandate-funding rule provides that any law or agency rule or regulation taking effect on or after January 1, 1981, which imposes additional costs on any city or town, is effective only if the Commonwealth assumes the cost. In the absence of state funding, the statute allows communities to comply voluntarily with a state mandate, but it does not require compliance. It does not, however, allow the community to make this decision on its own. The state auditor, for that matter, cannot make a decision that a law will be ineffective due to lack of state funding. He or she cannot because of the separation-of-powers doctrine. Only the judicial branch can declare an act of the legislature to be ineffective.

Accordingly, the local mandate law allows an aggrieved city or town to petition Superior Court for declaratory relief. The court may order that the complaining city or town be exempted from having to comply with the law or regulation if, in fact, the court agrees with the allegations. In one such case, the state Supreme Court exempted municipalities from having to carry out more private-school transportation responsibilities than they were previously required. This is known as the Lexington[3] decision, discussed below.

One section of Proposition 2½ created DLM. It is a new division within the state auditor's office. The law requires the division to review any post-1980 law or regulation that a municipality suggests is imposing new costs and to determine the amount of that cost. In any litigation, the amount of the cost imposed, as determined by DLM, would be prima facie evidence of the amount of state funding that would be necessary to sustain the mandate.

By the express terms of the statute, it might appear that the work is limited to providing evidence for mandate litigation. But, in practice, more has to be done because DLM cannot determine the amount of a cost imposed before it determines that there is truly a new obligation on a city or town that meets the elements of a mandate finding. DLM is very strict about this procedure because it is important to the auditor that he not be seen necessarily as a municipal advocate or as a state advocate. Toward that end, the office goes through a rather painstaking process in making decisions.

Note that the statute only allows a city or town to submit written notice DLM to ask for a mandate ruling. This provision does not include regional school districts, other regional entities, or counties. The statute is so written, and the statute is what governs the work.

Even though DLM's decision is not necessarily final, it has to come to a firm conclusion that there is, in fact, a new cost imposed on a community. Upon proper petition from a city or town, it looks for the elements of a mandate finding. In doing so, it establishes that the regulation or law was, in fact, effective on or after January 1, 1981. Then it determines that there is a cost imposed and that there has been no appropriation by the Commonwealth to assume the cost. Determining that there is, in fact, a cost imposed on a city or town by the law or regulation is often the most difficult part of the legal determination to be made. Clearly, as DLM sees them, conditional grants—compliance conditions that would be prerequisite to receiving a state grant—would not be costs imposed by the Commonwealth. They would not because a municipality would have a way to avoid the expense. If the city or town does not wish to perform this service, then it may decline the grant. Local option or the ability of a community to rescind prior acceptance of a law would defeat a mandate finding. This point can be made even when it is difficult for a city or town to decline local acceptance. An example is the recent amendments to the state Workers Compensation Act that imposed many new costs on communities. In the final analysis, even though realistically no community is going to rescind its acceptance of the Workers Compensation Act, that option was there. Court authority requires this type of interpretation. DLM calls it the *Lexington* hard choices doctrine.[4] It would be a hard choice and sometimes an impossible one as far as labor negotiations go to rescind acceptance of the Workers Compensation Act or many other local option programs. But there is that choice. And the State Supreme Court in the *Lexington* decision stated that when there is such choice, there is not a mandate within the meaning of the statute.

Another interesting point from the *Lexington* decision provides that when DLM determines whether a state appropriation has been made to assume the cost of any given new program, undesignated increases in general local aid will not satisfy. DLM has to find a specific appropriation for that specific program within the state budget.

Like most states, Massachusetts has several exceptions to the mandate-funding rule. By statute, there is an explicit exception for costs imposed by a court decision or costs imposed by a law or regulation adopted as a direct result of a court decision. With this in mind, mandate scrutiny has to include a review of all relevant court decisions on a given topic to ensure that the court exception/exclusion does not apply in any given case.

By interpretation, DLM also makes exceptions for federal pass-through laws and regulations. An example is the federal Handicapped Accessibility to Polling Places Act and accompanying state regulations. In the final analysis, DLM concluded that state regulations implementing the act required no more than was required by the federal law. Accordingly, there was no new state-mandated cost. Although it is sometimes difficult to draw the line, DLM finds in favor of a municipality if a *state* regulation imposes costs beyond the federal requirement.

Also by interpretation, DLM makes exceptions for laws that regulate private industry and indirectly increase the costs of running municipal government. An example is the recent Solid Waste Management Act, a major initiative in Massachusetts, whereby private owners and operators of certain solid-waste facilities had to make expensive environmental protection improvements to their equipment. The result is increased tipping fees for municipalities. Nonetheless, DLM concluded—again trying to be just as fair to the state as it is to the cities and towns—that this tipping-fee increase resulted more from the contractual relationship with the facility than from the state statute. Law or regulation must be found to impose the cost on a city or town before state funding obligations attach.

Generally, the Massachusetts mandate statute applies to all types of laws. They include educational, environmental, and public-safety laws, but *not* laws regulating the benefits of municipal employment. At the same time Proposition 2½ was enacted, the voters also adopted an amendment to the Massachusetts constitution; it provides that the types of laws regulating the wages, hours, benefits, and conditions of municipal employment can be imposed against municipalities if there is a two-thirds vote of each branch of the legislature.[5]

The Massachusetts mandate law requires state funding for even meritorious programs. This requirement is contrary to Janet Kelly's observations on South Carolina (see chapter 6). Some South Carolina officials seem not to mind social-policy state mandates—they do not complain about costs for new programs they see as justifiable. In Massachusetts, local officials seek reimbursement even when they agree with the policy behind a new mandate. They have this statutory right. If the legislators want to implement a statewide policy and it is important enough to them, they will have to find the money to fund it. This attitude fits into the economic context in which the local-mandate statute was created. Massachusetts cities and towns are restrained by Proposition 2½. They cannot raise additional revenues to support even meritorious programs. So the legislature has to put its money where its mouth is.

Generally, if DLM establishes the elements of a mandate finding with no exceptions, it begins the cost-documentation process, first with the individual petitioners. It then makes statewide estimates. (For more details, see chapter 9.)

The effects of a mandate determination under the Massachusetts statute are varied. On clear issues when the auditor finds a state mandate, the legislative response is generally positive. It is on clear issues in which the legal arguments are straightforward and the price tag is not too high. DLM communicates its findings to legislative leaders, and very often the funds are appropriated. The legislators benefit by saving their constituent communities the expense and time of litigation.

Other times, particularly on expensive items, legislators are reluctant to fund DLM determinations until an issue is decided in court. One landfill-related matter has been pending for three years. Throughout this period, several legislators whose constituent communities are affected by this new landfill regulation have filed bills to fund the costs imposed upon their communities as determined by DLM. But, in each case, the funding bills were defeated during the floor debate pending court determination of the issues. This controversy is currently pending before the Massachusetts Supreme Court.

When there is a no-mandate finding, a community still has the opportunity to go to court and challenge DLM's decision. But that has not happened yet. No-mandate determinations are turned over to a DLM section known as the Sunset Program.[6] It has authority to make recommendations concerning any law, even if it was effective before 1981. In this way, DLM can offer some further level of review for municipalities. Even if a law does not require state funding in the strict sense, DLM tries to determine whether the law may be unreasonable or should be modified in some other way.

A mandate-reimbursement law like the Massachusetts version provides a reasonable balance between the interests of local and state policymakers. There is a general expectation that mandated programs will be state funded. This feeling provides more independent decision-making authority for local budgetmakers who must work within the limits of Propostion 2½. On the other hand, strategies are available to the legislature for implementing statewide policy initiatives affecting local spending.

Should the legislature specifically desire, it can override the local mandate-funding rule. It can include explicit language in any law providing that a new service must be funded by municipalities, notwithstanding the provision of the local mandate law. The legislature has not yet exercised this option.

New programs can be imposed as irresistible conditions to state-aid distributions. This provision is a twist on the *Lexington* private-school transportation case. After the court held that communities no longer had to provide certain unfunded mandated transportation services, the legislature attached a proviso to the local aid item that has traditionally given state aid for several kinds of transportation: regular transportation, bilingual, and so forth. Any community that did not furnish private-school transportation would not receive its general school-transportation aid—truly an irresistible condition, because it involved large sums of money for most communities. Nonetheless, the court concluded that imposing such a condition was within the prerogative of the legislature.

DLM is seeing a growing use of local-option legislation, particularly in the property-tax-exemption areas. Quite often, the Ways and Means Committees call the office, and after discussing a matter, they amend a bill to include local option language. The DLM staff is pleased when that happens, because some say that this exchange is really what Proposition 2½ is all about, giving more decision-making power to the local level of government.

Few laws have passed since 1980 without some discussion of the local mandate issue if a matter impacts local government. The auditor's decisions are often quoted during house and senate floor debates. And local officials rely heavily upon DLM to continue this kind of work. Again, the state auditor's office is an important factor in having made it possible for municipalities to live within the limits of Proposition 2½.

The legislature is keenly aware that the local mandate-funding rule was a voter initiative. It knows now that if it does not stick with its part of this bargain, the citizens can go back to the polls and give them an even more stringent local mandate statute that they would have to live with.

Several states are doing just that. The Massachusetts mandate law is not a constitutional amendment, so the legislature has some leeway. And, states may want to consider this point as a defensive measure. Of course, no legislature would voluntarily bind itself to a mandate-funding rule. But, if states at least take some steps up front to ease the burden of costs imposed on local governments, they may find themselves in a better position to resist what might be a citizens' initiative to require funding of any statewide policy.

Notes

1. St. 1980, c.580 provides that property taxes assessed in any city or town may not exceed 2½ percent of the total full and fair cash value of taxable property within the town. This sum is capped at 102.5 percent of the maximum levy limit of the municipality in the prior fiscal year.

2. At the November 1986 state election, Massachusetts voters approved a measure limiting the allowable growth in state tax revenues to the average growth in wages and salaries over the prior three years. Any excess raised over allowable revenues must be refunded to income taxpayers. See M.G.L. c.62F.

3. Town of Lexington v. Commissioner of Education, 393 Mass. 693 (1985).

4. Town of Lexington v. Commissioner of Education, 397 Mass. 593 (1986).

5. See Massachusetts Constitution, 115th Article of Amendment.

6. M.G.L. c.11, s.6B

Chapter Nine

COST ESTIMATION AND REIMBURSEMENT OF MANDATES

Anthony V. D'Aiello

OVERVIEW

The Massachusetts Division of Local Mandates (DLM) is placed within the Office of the State Auditor, headed by an independent elected official. Its genesis is important because it means that DLM's rulings on whether post-1980 state laws, rules, and regulations violate Proposition 2½ and the local mandate statute[1] and should therefore be state funded are impartial. If the state requirements are based on pre-1981 authority, allow for local acceptance, or stem from court orders or federal mandates, then the local mandate statute does not apply.

It also means that DLM's determination of the expenses municipalities incur or anticipate due to state-mandated programs are calculated accurately and fairly. For example, financial-cost models are used to compute the estimated costs of pending legislation and draft state regulations. In addition, the anticipated cost savings a particular proposed or effective law or regulation may generate for cities and towns are considered, when appropriate, in arriving at the state's net funding obligation. For unfunded state programs already in effect, DLM requires municipalities to submit cost documentation, such as bill receipts, payroll data, cost quotes, and so on, as evidence that expenses were incurred or are anticipated. In other instances, a cost claim form is forwarded to local officials, who are then asked to detail incremental state-mandated expenditures and to sign a verification clause to attest that the costs are genuine.

In summary, DLM believes that the way to maintain the respect and credibility of both state and local officials is to continue issuing sound, impartial legal rulings on the applicability of the local mandate law to state-mandated programs, to employ the latest in computer cost-modeling techniques to estimate potential statewide costs, and to require verification of mandated expenses from municipal officials.

As DLM strives toward these ends, more and more legislative committees and state agencies are contacting DLM before the fact—before promulgating costly laws and regulations. Today, DLM frequently works with these state officials to help draft new state programs that will be consistent with the local mandate law. It also provides them with statewide cost studies that identify the financial impacts proposed unfunded laws and regulations would have on municipalities. This practice is consistent with the auditor's proactive stance, seeking consensus to fund state-mandated programs in the initial proposal stages.

UP-FRONT FUNDING VERSUS REIMBURSEMENT

An important interpretation of the local mandate provisions of Proposition 2½ is found in a 1985 Massachusetts Supreme Judicial Court decision, *Town of Lexington v. Commissioner of Education.*[2] The state's highest court ruled that laws are ineffective when they are enacted without provisions for state assumption of local costs in each year the costs are imposed. The decision also stated that this funding should come in the form of up-front monies.

Nevertheless, new state programs continue to become effective without this state funding commitment. Although exact numbers are hard to come by, DLM has an overall sense that these instances are decreasing because of its increasing participation in the preliminary stages of enacting new state programs. Surprisingly, more and more legislators and state agency heads are complying with this spirit of Proposition 2½, for it can result in the smooth local implementation of programs important to them, while avoiding the risk of DLM's determining that the program is subject to the local mandate law and the courts' ruling them ineffective. This latter ruling would essentially exempt municipalities from the mandated provisions until state funding is provided, and provided up front.

In short, DLM's position and, naturally, that of local officials, is that state funding should be appropriated for each mandated activity and it should be up front so communities do not have to appropriate and expend limited financial resources in anticipation of state reimbursements later. For this reason, provisions of the local mandate law were incorporated into Proposition 2½ to balance the fiscal constraints Proposition 2½ placed on local governments' property tax revenue-raising capabilities.

UP-FRONT FUNDING PROCESS

In keeping with its proactive stance, DLM follows legislation through a computer-tracking system tied into the legislature's computer system. More than 6,000 pieces of legislation are reviewed by staff yearly for mandate implications. "Big ticket" unfunded mandate bills are pulled out and action is taken. Hundreds of proposed regulations are also reviewed yearly.

DLM legal staff checks that the bills would in fact impose new financial impacts on cities and towns. The research unit then attempts to attach a price tag to the legislation. It does so by sampling 40 cities and towns representative of the entire state in terms of population and other demographic variables. The survey instruments are concise and not burdensome to local officials, so that local cost data can be quickly gathered and tabulated. DLM also creates computer-cost models to calculate the numbers and to translate them on a statewide basis for 351 cities and towns over a three-year period. Future-year costs are sometimes tabulated using inflation factors. Public and private sectors provide other relevant information and cost data. For instance, if unit costs for mandated equipment purchases can be obtained from private-sector sources, this information can be plugged into the cost model and statewide costs computed in a matter of seconds, without going the survey route. DLM sometimes works with legislative committees and state agency officials in a combined effort to cost out proposed mandated programs.

DLM's legislative unit then takes over, contacting legislative committees and state agencies and advising them of DLM's concerns and cost findings. Ideally, a consensus is formed that the new program requires a state funding commitment, and either the funding is appropriated and provided to communities up front so that local finances are not affected, or the program is not mandated.

This system has worked on several issues. The 1984 suicide prevention law[3] required in part that local lockups make their jail cells suicide proof. DLM advised the legislature—based on information received from local police chiefs and their association—that this proposition was expensive, that it would require more than the $1 million reimbursement appropriated for renovation costs. A total of

$10 million was soon appropriated and has been provided to cities and towns on an up-front basis by the Governor's Office for Administration and Finance.

In 1983, DLM reviewed an added-polling-hours bill that, in effect, mandated cities and towns to keep their polling precincts open an additional three hours for state elections.[4] Through a representative sampling of communities, DLM projected the statewide added-personnel and other fixed costs, (e.g., rent, heating, and lighting) that the bill would impose on cities and towns. A funding commitment was soon added to the bill, and the legislature authorized DLM to certify local costs for each election. As a result, since 1984, $3 million has been provided to cities and towns in up-front monies for election costs.

DLM also identified a 1984 right-to-know bill as potentially costly mandate legislation. A quick survey estimated statewide costs. DLM presented its findings to the legislature, and since then, nearly $1 million in up-front monies has been made available to local officials for costs incurred complying with the environmental investigative and reporting requirements of the new law.[5] In handling this funding issue, the executive branch is using an up-front funding vehicle that forwards cities and towns per-capita monies that are then drawn down on a quarterly basis, providing that local governments give an account to the governor's office on how the money is spent. DLM considers this mechanism an ideal way of satisfying the funding requirements of the local mandate law.

In 1986, DLM assisted the legislature and the Department of Education in estimating three-year costs for the school breakfast bill.[6] Through survey information and by deducting federal funding for school breakfast expenses, DLM estimated costs for affected school systems. Today, about $710,000 has been targeted in up-front state funding.

A final example is a 1987 bill[7] that would have required local police agencies to pay for enrolling their part-time police in full-time police-officer-training courses. Based on information gathered from the Executive Office of Public Safety and through surveys, DLM estimated these costs at nearly $25 million. The bill was refiled in 1988, but again it did not pass, given the costs involved.

In short, by getting involved early in the process and by establishing positive relationships with state officials, DLM can ensure that state funding is provided before, not after, the fact, and can ensure that, in any case, it is provided.

THE REIMBURSEMENT PROCESS

In reality, new mandated programs become effective without state funding. The local fiscal impact is not considered until local officials begin compliance. These local officials turn to DLM when they are faced with mandated costs they have not anticipated and budgeted for. Then DLM's role is to determine what affected municipalities have spent or expect to spend. As mentioned above, verifiable proof is required of incurred or anticipated expenses. DLM's determination of this amount can then be submitted in court as prima facie evidence in suits brought by cities and towns to seek an exemption from the mandate until state funding is provided.

During DLM's cost-documentation process, DLM attempts to determine the statewide costs imposed. This process enables DLM to recommend to state agencies or to the legislature the amount of reimbursement necessary not only for one petitioning community but for all 351 cities and towns. The process may require municipal officials to submit cost documentation or complete signed cost claim forms. DLM's job then is to make its findings available to the legislature and state agencies with the hope that state reimbursement will be appropriated and distributed to affected cities and towns.

An example of how this system works was in 1986, when the legislature enacted the Race and Primary Language law.[8] This unfunded statute required a new one-time census taken by municipal census officials. They were to identify and report to the Secretary of State the race and primary language of residents. Through cost claim forms and by unit costs gathered from private computer service bureaus for new census lists, DLM determined statewide costs that it presented to the state agency. The state agency then requested and was granted an appropriation of $900,000 to reimburse the expenses incurred by cities and towns, as certified by DLM.

A last example is the 1983 State Department of Public Health ambulance service regulations,[9] which were promulgated without state funding. Today the legislature still reimburses affected cities and towns for past costs. These costs are first gathered and certified by DLM.

ROADBLOCKS TO SUCCESS

Concerns are raised when the legislature pays for the mandates it imposes on cities and towns out of the local aid fund. This fund, officials believe, should be state revenues shared with local officials without any strings attached; they should not be used to fund mandates. When the economy of the state is less than healthy, legislators and the executive branch may not be inclined to agree with DLM to fund new state-mandated programs.

Massachusetts experienced tremendous revenue growth during the 1980s. However, a recent trend of spending growth in excess of revenue growth, along with severe revenue shortfalls, has created a structural revenue-spending gap, which has existed for at least three years. Consequently, the governor and legislative leaders are considering both temporary and permanent new taxes, among other measures, to assist in balancing the FY 1989 and FY 1990 budgets. Given the state's new fiscal reality, FY 1990 budget proposals call for a reduction in direct local aid. Total local aid (comprised of direct and indirect aid, lottery aid, and resolution aid) almost doubled from FY 1983 to FY 1989 ($2.1 billion to $3.9 billion). But proposed FY 1990 total local aid will increase only 2 percent or $83 million from FY 1989, in contrast to average yearly increases of 11 percent (an average of $297 million yearly).

This anticipated downturn in infusions of state financial assistance, along with an overall decline since 1981 of property tax revenues brought about by Proposition 2½, has led the legislature to propose further modification of Proposition 2½. One proposal would allow city councils and town meetings by a two-thirds vote to assess property taxes for debt service outside the limits of Proposition 2½ without obtaining voter approval. Also in 1987, Chapter 229 of the Acts of 1987 allowed communities to pass an override of Proposition 2½ to increase general revenues with a simple majority vote, instead of the previously required two-thirds voter approval. However, less than half the Proposition-2½-override attempts in the state's 351 cities and towns have been successful, even with this less-restrictive override provision.

Sometimes legislators and state officials label DLM as a roadblock to successful local implementation of important state programs because it raises the mandate issue. Although the merits of a new law or regulation are commendable, cities and towns must be assisted in paying for them, especially today, given state and municipal financial problems. DLM has thus increased its efforts to provide state policymakers with timely local cost impacts of proposed state programs. As a result, these officials are far more reluctant to pass costly local mandates.

Another roadblock can be gathering cost data from part-time officials of small communities. Of the 351 cities and towns in Massachusetts, 123 towns have less than 5,000 residents. However, because input from these local officials is needed, for it is these small towns that most often feel the biggest negative impact from state mandates, DLM keeps in constant contact with them through its field services staff, and designs surveys and cost claim forms that are quick and easy to complete.

FACTORS AFFECTING DLM's SUCCESS

DLM staff has varied and experienced backgrounds. Some are also part-time town clerks, selectmen, city councilors, and assessing officers. One was a three-term mayor. Some have worked in other municipal and state agencies. Many have, or are working toward, law and master's degrees. They also participate in courses and seminars intended to further educational and professional careers.

Another factor contributing to DLM success is its field services and legislative liaison units. DLM has established positive working relationships with local officials and their various municipal associations, legislators, and state agency staff. As a result, DLM receives about 500 written inquiries a year concerning state-mandated programs from local and state officials. It also responds to about 600 phone calls annually, providing information and assistance to municipal and state officials, and reviews and certifies hundreds of cost claim forms and surveys yearly for state funding.

Another factor contributing to DLM effectiveness is the continuing refinement of its computer cost model. The data bank and cost-modeling techniques are more advanced than those of most state agencies. Costing out mandates is as much an art as a science—there are relatively few rules to follow. DLM staff is given considerable leeway for judgment and for coming up with innovative methods of cost analysis and estimation. All activities are accomplished on an annual budget of $860,000.

DLM work is easier when the legislature completes its own estimates on the local costs of legislation. It is also easier when the executive branch fulfills the intent of the Governor's Executive Order 145, which requires state agency heads to estimate the municipal fiscal impacts of the regulations they propose. Given the author's personal experience, there continues to be a need for DLM. It will not become extinct for lack of unfunded state mandates proposed or enacted.

CONCLUSION

Since DLM's beginning in 1983, nearly $20 million in state funding has been provided to cities and towns for mandated requirements, either up front or in reimbursements. More important, millions of other dollars in potential state-imposed costs were not imposed because of concerns DLM raised. DLM intends to continue meeting its objectives.

Notes

1. M.G.L. c. 29, s. 27C.
2. Town of Lexington v. Commissioner of Education, 393 Mass. 693 (1985).
3. M.G.L. c. 40, s. 36B.
4. Chapter 503 of the Acts of 1983.
5. Chapter 470 of the Acts of 1983.
6. Chapter 356 of the Acts of 1986.
7. House No. 84.
8. Chapter 165 of the Acts of 1985.
9. 105 CMR 170 et seq.

Chapter Ten

CONNECTICUT'S CONSIDERATION AND REJECTION OF A MANDATE REIMBURSEMENT PROGRAM

Geary Maher

Connecticut has exhibited great caution with regard to the mandatory reimbursement concept. A phrase that perhaps summarizes Connecticut's experience with this concept is the rise and fall of the reimbursement issue in the land of steady habits.

About seven years ago, the state began to seriously consider the adoption of a mandatory reimbursement program but, after a year and a half of careful consideration, decided against it.

Some background information outlining the responsibilities of the Office of Fiscal Analysis and the emergence of the state mandates issue in Connecticut is important as a background for understanding Connecticut's reluctance.

The office of fiscal analysis (OFA), the legislature's budget office, consists of 20 professionals who handle the following three major responsibilities:

☐ Assisting the two fiscal committees (Appropriations and Finance) in the formulation of their budgetary recommendations to the full legislature.
☐ Researching fiscal issues for any of the 187 legislators who might ask for assistance (although OFA works primarily for the fiscal committees).
☐ Preparing state and municipal fiscal impact statements (fiscal notes) on legislation. OFA analysts append a fiscal note to each bill favorably reported by nonfiscal committees. The bill, along with the fiscal note, is then distributed to all members of the house and senate. In addition, analysts provide preliminary fiscal notes on bills being seriously considered by the fiscal committees before these bills are favorably reported. OFA analysts complete approximately 2,000–3,000 fiscal notes per year on bills, amendments, and amended bills. It began preparing state fiscal notes in the mid-1970s and started

providing municipal fiscal notes in 1979. The work on municipal fiscal notes exposes OFA to the state mandates issue.

Interest in the possibility of adopting state mandates legislation in Connecticut was spurred by passage of legislation around 1978 regarding hypertension benefits for local police and firemen. The legislation passed before OFA started preparing municipal fiscal-impact statements; it had serious cost implications for municipalities that became apparent once the legislation was implemented.

Several organizations that represent municipalities were sensitive to the legislation and pushed for a legislative remedy to avoid this type of development in the future. Some form of reimbursement was suggested for state mandates. These organizations joined forces with a legislator from a rural community who believed philosophically that the state should bear at least part of the costs associated with imposing mandates on municipalities.

As a result of this concern, the State Mandates Interim Study Committee, composed of five members of the Appropriations Committee, was established pursuant to 1983 legislation.[1] The committee is required to report on the feasibility of a pilot program for reimbursing municipalities for the cost of new or expanded state mandates.

Connecticut's cautious approach is evident in this 1983 legislation. A mandatory reimbursement program would be considered, but any implementation would occur on a limited pilot basis within one specific program area of government. Implementing the pilot program in the environment/economic development area of government was subsequently considered. The 1983 legislation also:

☐ Defined state mandate as "any state-initiated constitutional, statutory or executive action that requires a local government to establish, expand or modify its activities in such a way as to necessitate additional expenditures from local revenues, excluding any order issued by a state court and any legislation necessary to comply with a federal mandate."

☐ Required OFA to prepare fiscal notes on state mandates. Because OFA had already been providing them since 1979, for practical purposes, analysts began indicating state mandate in capital letters on the fiscal note to alert legislators to the existence of legislation that would impose a state mandate.

☐ Required OFA to review state mandates and the cost of such mandates passed during the 1983 legislative session. Approximately 40 out of the 800 bills passed were identified as state mandates.

☐ Defined various types of mandates and other conditions related to the mandates (e.g., disclaimers that were conditions under which the state would not provide reimbursement if a reimbursement procedure had been subsequently enacted) and required that the types of mandates and related conditions be indicated on fiscal notes. This requirement was subsequently repealed through 1984 legislation.

The next year, the State Mandates Interim Study Committee thoroughly researched the issue, with a thrust toward establishing a pilot-reimbursement program in 1984 in the environment/economic development area of government. In the process of its deliberations, there was an effort to:

☐ collect comparative information from other states especially California and Illinois regarding their reimbursement programs,
☐ identify costs that would be reimbursed and the timetable for reimbursement,
☐ improve OFA's ability to get more complete information from municipalities on a timely basis (e.g., developing a contact list of up to 10 small, medium, and large municipalities out of the total 169 cities and towns in Connecticut), and
☐ assess the administrative costs associated with instituting a reimbursement procedure in Connecticut.

Although most of the study committee's efforts centered on devising an elaborate scheme of reimbursement that would have been implemented on a pilot basis, the ultimate legislation that passed did not go that far, and only relatively modest legislation was enacted in 1984. Connecticut's reluctance can be attributed to the following types of issues that were not completely resolved:

☐ how to define reimbursable costs (e.g., should reimbursements include indirect as well as direct costs)?
☐ which timetable for reimbursement should be chosen (e.g., provide reimbursement in the first year or wait two or three years until the overall impact becomes more evident), what amount of reimbursement should be provided (e.g., institute a percentage share arrangement with municipalities), and whether the reimbursement should be phased in (e.g., 25 percent for the first year, 50 percent for the second year, etc.)?
☐ should the state provide reimbursement for mandates requested by municipalities or for those mandates already in place?

□ how to ensure that quality data could be obtained quickly from cities and towns and how to obtain reasonable fiscal estimates given that municipalities do not often know initially how a proposed mandate will be implemented?

□ how much money should be spent by the state reviewing, processing, and auditing claims and establishing an appeals board to resolve complaints (annually, Illinois and California were spending approximately $50,000 and $750,000, respectively, to support the administrative components of their state mandates program, and Connecticut was not only hesitant about incurring these additional costs but was also unwilling to establish this layer of bureaucracy), and

□ reluctance on the part of the Appropriations Committee chairs and other legislative leaders to give up some control over expenditures by instituting a mandatory reimbursement procedure due to the state's uncertain fiscal condition at the time.

The following two reactions to some extent typify Connecticut's cautiousness with regard to adopting a mandatory reimbursement procedure. The Appropriations Committee chair had serious concerns about relinquishing some control over state appropriations to an automatic reimbursement mechanism; she often questioned whether the mandatory-reimbursement approach made sense and whether the state's best interests would be served by moving in that direction.

In addition, one highly respected Connecticut state auditor, who has held several important positions in state government, expressed his concerns as follows:

As you know, I don't think this concept makes any sense. Further, assuming acceptance of the concept, the method of dealing with it as proposed in the working draft is crazy.

The draft [legislation] raises so many questions that it is unproductive to go through them in this memo . . . .

The process of computing the costs consistently among all the local government entities and setting up the procedures, staff and timetable for OPM [the Governor's budget office] to approve requests and hear appeals would be a nightmare . . . .

If there is a compulsion to proceed with this concept, I think that each bill establishing or expanding a mandate should include an appropriation and a formula for distributing the appropriations. The Assembly [state legislature] would have the choice of adopting or removing the appropriation . . . .[2]

As a result of the technical implementation problems that were identified but not completely resolved and the concerns expressed by some legislative officials, Connecticut began to consider more seriously a voluntary rather than mandatory reimbursement scheme. In lieu of a mandatory reimbursement procedure being enacted in 1984 on a pilot basis with regard to the state's environment/development programs, a voluntary reimbursement procedure was adopted.

After a year and a half of careful consideration, legislation was enacted in 1984. It requires that any bills creating or enlarging state mandates be referred to the Appropriations Committee.[3] The statute requires that any such bill that is favorably reported by the Appropriations Committee contain a determination concerning:

☐ whether such bill creates or enlarges a state mandate, and if so, which type of mandate is created or enlarged and
☐ whether the state shall reimburse local governments for costs resulting from such new or enlarged mandate, and if so, which costs are eligible for reimbursement and the level of, timetable for, and duration of reimbursement.

The Appropriations Committee provided these determinations in the first year but has not done so subsequently as interest in the state mandates issue has declined. No direct reimbursement has ever been provided through this legislation. Bills that would impose state mandates are still referred to the Appropriations Committee; however, the general issue and the potential for reimbursing municipalities for new or expanded mandates imposed by the state have received relatively little attention in the last three to four years.

It is somewhat difficult to measure the effectiveness of Connecticut's state mandates law. Perhaps the law has reduced the number of additional mandates being imposed by making legislators more aware of the consequences of their actions on municipalities. Fewer such bills seem to be introduced, and even fewer are given serious consideration and eventually passed. Most bills affecting municipalities that pass do not impose significant burdens and often create relatively simple administrative changes that usually result in either no cost or minimal municipal costs that can be absorbed.

In addition, immediate attention was diverted from the mandates issue because the fiscal pressures on Connecticut's state and local governments that existed prior to passage of the state mandates legislation were temporarily alleviated. The state enjoyed sizable general fund surpluses totaling $1.146 billion over four consecutive fiscal years as follows: $165.2 million for 1983–84, $365.5 million for 1984–85, $250.1 million for 1985–86, and $365.2 million for 1986–87. In lieu of funding any new state mandates or directly funding existing ones, Connecticut was in a better financial position to provide more indirect assistance to municipalities through general state aid, including property tax relief grants. As a result of the improved fiscal condition of the state, legislative and municipal officials became less concerned about direct reimbursement for specific state mandates.

This attitude could change, however, if the state's fiscal picture continues to worsen in future years. Connecticut ended FY 1987–88 with a $115.6 million deficit and FY 1988–89 with a $28.0 million deficit, and increased taxes and slowed the rate of growth in expenditures to avert a deficit in 1989–90. Although the 1989–90 budget either reduces or slows the rate of growth in some grants to municipalities, overall state aid continues to increase. Table 10.1 indicates the appropriated level of state aid to municipalities from FY 1982–83 through FY 1989–90.

As a result of continued increases in state aid to municipalities despite the more recent worsening in the overall fiscal condition, the sensitivity associated with the state mandates-reimbursement issue has not reemerged. However, if state and municipal resources become strained by more intense fiscal pressure, a renewed interest in terms of reconsidering a mandatory-reimbursement mechanism could result.

It is ironic, however, that although Connecticut was in a good financial position from 1983–84 to 1986–87 to reimburse specific mandates, it chose not to do so. Instead, the state opted to provide more indirect assistance to cities and towns by increasing state aid

Table 10.1 CONNECTICUT'S AID TO MUNICIPALITIES: ALL APPROPRIATED FUNDS, FY 1982–83 TO FY 1989–90

Fiscal Year	Amount	Increase	Percent Increase
1982–83	$ 667,333,259	$ 52,258,120	8.50%
1983–84	747,036,140	79,702,881	11.94
1984–85	836,353,011	89,316,871	11.96
1985–86	905,527,991	69,174,980	8.27
1986–87	1,058,987,397	153,459,406	16.95
1987–88	1,155,538,857	96,551,460	9.12
1988–89	1,297,171,601	141,632,744	12.26
1989–90	1,397,944,189	100,772,588	7.77

to municipalities. Now that the state is in a more difficult fiscal situation, resources may be too limited to provide reimbursement for specific mandates. If the fiscal situation deteriorates further, it might become increasingly difficult to enact a mandatory reimbursement procedure in Connecticut.

Notes

1. P.A. 83-12 (June Special Session), An Act Concerning State Mandates to Local Governments.

2. State Auditor Leo V. Donohue's memorandum to Representative Janet Polinsky, Chair of the Appropriations Committee, January 1984.

3. P.A. 84-124, An Act Establishing Procedures with Respect to Bills Creating or Enlarging State Mandates Which May Result in Costs to Local Governments.

Chapter Eleven

ALTERNATIVES TO FEDERAL MANDATE REIMBURSEMENT FROM THE PERSPECTIVE OF THE CONGRESSIONAL BUDGET OFFICE

James L. Blum

The costs that can be imposed by federal mandates on state and local governments have led to an effort to focus on such costs before legislation is passed.[1] Current proposals to highlight the costs of federal mandates generally fall into three areas:

☐ More information could be produced on the costs of federal mandates, the flow of information could be improved, and such information could have a more significant role in the legislative process.
☐ State and local governments and their representative organizations could present their concerns to Congress more effectively.
☐ The legislative process could be revised to focus more attention on federal mandates. For example, the process could include procedural roadblocks on new legislation that would impose large unfunded costs on state and local governments.

At this stage, the most fruitful and appropriate step is the second area. If state and local governments want the costs of federal mandates to be taken more seriously, they should devote more resources to tracking proposed legislation and regulations.

IMPROVING THE AVAILABILITY OF INFORMATION

Information about the cost even of existing federal mandates is generally not informative because definitions of the concepts involved vary widely. In 1984, a report on regulatory federalism by the ACIR called for "additional sound research on the effects of federal mandates."[2] Such research is an obvious first step if future federal mandates are to be challenged on the basis of cost, but the research faces considerable hurdles in terms of establishing data and method, and it will be time consuming.

CBO could expand its efforts to prepare state and local cost estimates. The estimates could be prepared earlier in the legislative process, at the subcommittee level; they could also be prepared for amendments offered on the floor of the House or for conference reports and distributed to organizations representing state and local governments. A CBO annual report could summarize all such estimates. But an increase in CBO efforts would not be cost effective unless there is a demand for the information being provided. Until now, demand has been isolated, and CBO has responded to the limited demand effectively. Committees and the state and local government interest groups have only rarely shown interest in CBO's cost estimates. In any case, the primary role of CBO is to serve the information needs of Congress and not those of particular interest groups. More state and local cost estimates prepared by CBO would not necessarily improve the flow of information or the quality of the estimates.

COMMUNICATING CONCERNS TO THE CONGRESS

A more effective presentation of the state and local case before legislation is passed would be another way of approaching the problem of federally mandated costs. Indeed, state and local organizations recently managed to achieve amendments to the Fair Labor Standards Act to avoid the added costs of the Supreme Court 1985 decision in the *Garcia* case.[3] However, state and local governments rarely focus on new legislation until after it has become law. For example, CBO received inquiries from the states only after the recent immigration reforms became law, despite the fact that these reforms were clearly going to impose significant costs at the state and local levels.

If state and local governments believe the problem of federal mandates is serious, then they should recognize the need to devote more of their own resources to the issue. For example, the organizations representing state and local governments could establish a central clearinghouse to track legislation that would affect them. This clearinghouse, which would not need to be large, could prepare its own annual report on the costs of federal legislation, based on CBO fiscal notes (cost estimates) as well as its own sources of information. The clearinghouse could eventually become a useful source of information for CBO in preparing cost estimates, and it could distribute CBO cost estimates to interested groups.

The Office of Management and Budget (OMB) and CBO receive their mandates from the president and Congress, and it is therefore inappropriate for state and local governments to expect their case to be represented from these quarters. The responsibility lies with the state and local governments to exert pressure on Congress on their own behalf. Congress and the president can then decide whether CBO and OMB should prepare more estimates on the costs of federal mandates.

ALTERING THE LEGISLATIVE PROCESS

Proposals to use the legislative process to draw attention to the costs of federal mandates fall into two major categories. First, federal reimbursement could be required for new federal mandates, such as in Senator Durenberger's proposed bill.[4] Second, any member of Congress could raise a point of order against a bill that imposes a cost of some stipulated amount or more on state and local governments— this is the gist of Congressman Barnard's bill.[5]

Federal reimbursement entails a number of problems: it is difficult to determine the actual costs of mandates, Congress could waive the reimbursement requirement, and costs incurred to date (but not yet reimbursed) would raise the question of the fair distribution of reimbursement funds. Often CBO cost estimates would not be a suitable basis for reimbursement because the costs cannot be accurately determined in advance. Only state and local governments can specify the costs that mandates impose on them, and most reimbursements should probably be based on these actual costs rather than cost projections. GAO could then audit and evaluate the actual costs reported by the state and local governments.

A new federal grant program to reimburse state and local governments could be proposed, to distribute funds on a formula basis along the lines of the now defunct general revenue-sharing program. A strong case would have to be made for such an expenditure, however, given the federal deficit problem. Once again, it seems that more research must be done to establish a firm basis for estimating the costs of existing mandates. The alternative approach to general reimbursement would be selective reimbursement in major areas, as for the Immigration Control and Legalization Amendments Act of 1986, which provided funds at the outset to help the states absorb the cost of that reform. State and local governments and their representatives would have to participate actively in this case-by-case approach, underlining the need for them to increase their involvement in the issue of federal mandate costs.

The procedural roadblocks suggested in Congressman Barnard's bill would place a considerable burden on CBO because the bill would rely on the CBO director to judge when a point of order might be raised. The bill would amend the House rules so that a member could raise a point of order against any bill that would create an unfunded mandate in excess of $50 million as estimated by CBO. This provision would require CBO to prepare estimates for all bills and amendments to make such a judgment and provide evidence for Congress to examine.

Apart from the huge amount of paperwork this procedure would create, a more important question is whether CBO, as a nonpartisan organization, should be placed so centrally in such a political process. The question of federal mandates and their costs is largely political, not technical. In other provisions for points of order in the Congressional Budget and Impoundment Control Act of 1974, the responsibility for providing budget estimates rests with the budget committees. Because the budget process is ultimately political, it would be more appropriate in the case of federal mandates to use a congressional committee for estimates on which points of order may be based.

CONSIDERING THE COSTS OF FEDERAL MANDATES

Both CBO and Congress could attempt to give more consideration to the costs of federal mandates at the state and local levels. However, as outlined above, there are many problems with the actions that CBO or Congress could take. More appropriate first steps could and should be taken by the state and local governments themselves, for it is their case that must be presented to Congress as legislation is debated. In combination with more research aimed at establishing common methods of cost estimation and data collection, a more aggressive approach by state and local governments earlier in the process of legislation would focus attention on the costs of federal mandates and allow them to receive the attention they deserve.

Notes

1. A study by Kee and Diehl provides an insightful analysis of this issue. See James Edwin Kee and William Diehl, "Assessing the Costs of Federal Mandates on State and Local Government" (draft, 1988).

2. Advisory Commission on Intergovernmental Relations, *Regulatory Federalism: Policy, Process, Impact and Reform* (Washington, D.C.: U.S. Government Printing Office, 1984), pp. 181–2.

3. In Garcia v. San Antonio Metropolitan Transit Authority (469 U.S. 528), the Supreme Court held that state and local governments were bound by the overtime compensation requirements of the Fair Labor Standards Act.

4. S. 585, The Intergovernmental Regulatory Relief Act of 1987, 100th Cong., 1st sess.

5. H.R. 1278, A bill to amend the Congressional Budget Act of 1974 to minimize the impact on state and local governments of unexpected provisions of legislation proposing the imposition of large unfunded costs on such governments, and for other purposes, 100th Cong., 1st sess.

ABOUT THE EDITORS

Michael Fix is a senior research associate at The Urban Institute. He is co-author of an early study of mandates for The Joint Economic Committee of Congress and of an assessment of the Reagan Administration's regulatory policies—*Relief or Reform: Reagan's Regulatory Dilemma.* He is currently completing a study of the implementation of 1986 Immigration Reform and Control Act.

Daphne A. Kenyon is an economics professor at Simmons College. From 1983-88 she was a researcher and public policy analyst specializing in issues of state and local public finance at the U.S. Advisory Commission on Intergovernmental Relations, the U.S. Treasury, and The Urban Institute. She is the author of studies of federal deductibility of state and local taxes, state fiscal discipline mechanisms, and interjurisdictional tax and policy competition.

ABOUT THE CONTRIBUTORS

Ann Calvaresi Barr is on a four-year appointment, begun in 1988, working on national security/defense and human rights issues in the General Accounting Office's European office in Frankfurt, West Germany. As a program evaluator with GAO, she worked for three years with the Intergovernmental Relations Group of the Human Resources Division.

David R. Beam is associate professor of public administration at Illinois Institute of Technology, where he directs its Master of Public Administration program. As senior analyst with the Advisory Commission on Intergovernmental Relations, he directed studies of regulatory federalism and the federal role in the federal system. His most recent book is *Taxing Choices: The Politics of Tax Reform.*

James L. Blum has been the assistant director for budget analysis at the Congressional Budget Office since 1975 when CBO was established. He also served as the acting director of CBO for 14 months in 1988–89. Previously, he worked for the Office of Management and Budget, the Department of Labor, the Council on Wage and Price Stability, and the Organization for Economic Co-operation and Development.

Anthony V. D'Aiello is manager of the Mandate Research Program at the Massachusetts State Auditor's Office, Division of Local Mandates. From 1983 to 1986, he was a research analyst at DLM.

Theresa A. Gullo is an analyst at the Congressional Budget Office where she prepares state and local government cost estimates and manages land and water resource issues in the Budget Analysis Division. With a background in public policy and intergovernmental finance, she was a research associate at The Urban Institute from 1983 to 1985, during which time she coauthored *The Reagan Block Grants: What Have We Learned.*

Richard H. Horte is assignment manager in the Human Resources Division of the General Accounting Office. Working with the division's Intergovernmental Relations Group, he is responsible for various assignments, especially those relating to federal block grants and federal regulatory policy, including the recent GAO study on legislative mandates.

Janet M. Kelly is a researcher at the College of Urban, Labor, and Metropolitan Affairs at Wayne State University. A public finance specialist, she was the economist for the South Carolina Advisory Commission on Intergovernmental Relations, working for two of her years there studying mandates in South Carolina.

Arnold M. Kuzmack is the director of the Program Development and Evaluation Division in the EPA Office of Drinking Water. He previously served in the EPA Office of Policy and Evaluation, the Brookings Institution, and the Office of the Secretary of Defense.

Emily D. Lunceford is chief counsel for the Massachusetts State Auditor's Office, Division of Local Mandates. She has served the Massachusetts General Court eight years in various capacities, primarily in the areas of educational law and finance.

Geary Maher is chief budget analyst for the Connecticut General Assembly's Office of Fiscal Analysis. He has worked closely with the Joint Committee on Appropriations since 1976 on a variety of issues including state mandates.